T0368169

CRUCIBLE:
Refining
Gold

What I learned
while Healing
from Childhood
TRAUMA.

JULIE CANNATA

WESTBOW
PRESS®
A DIVISION OF THOMAS NELSON
& ZONDERVAN

WestBow Press books may be ordered through booksellers or by contacting:

WestBow Press
A Division of Thomas Nelson & Zondervan
1663 Liberty Drive
Bloomington, IN 47403
www.westbowpress.com
844-714-3454

ISBN: 979-8-3850-1599-3 (sc)
ISBN: 979-8-3850-1598-6 (e)

Library of Congress Control Number: 2023924720

Print information available on the last page.

WestBow Press rev. date: 02/26/2024

ACKNOWLEDGMENTS

A sincere and humble thank you to my husband, Geno. His love and patience endure through this journey we continue to travel hand in hand. Thanks to my beautiful children, their loving support has encouraged me through the turbulence that is: Healing a traumatic past.

I am overflowing with tenderness for the loyalty and love of my steadfast younger siblings, who accepted me as I evolved, and who I would help raise, foster, cherish, and nurture all over again.

Special blessings to my 'ROOT FRIENDS', they have stood the test of time. Their prayers and presence have sustained me through my darkest moments.

Heartfelt appreciation to Matthew Gallagher, my Trauma Therapist. Thank you for your expertise and energy spent helping me survive this fight for my life.

FORWARD

After years of struggling with depression, anxiety, headaches, and sleepless nights, Julie discovered the early childhood abuse her mind protected her from remembering. She didn't ask to remember this, but like so many others who have suffered early childhood trauma it slowly emerged through episodes of treatment. Trauma survivors often struggle with conflicted feelings of insecurity, anger, self-loathing, denial, (and many others) that impact their ability to function and stress their relationships. This second book chronicles Julie's effort to cling to her faith, repair relationships, and accept loss. Like so many other areas of life, she approached her treatment with fierce determination. It reads like a passionate devotional illustrating her struggle to rediscover hope after setbacks and make peace with this new imperfect yet wholly acceptable sense of self, she has consistently expressed her desire to redeem her experience by helping others, and in that spirit, this book will resonate with individuals confronting their own shadows and empower those struggling with doubt. Whatever you say about Julie, or hear her say about herself, she is authentic in her concern for those around her and, like all of us, seeks the same acceptance for herself.

Matthew Gallagher, LCPC

PREFACE

Life throws us curve balls constantly. Some, like me, have no idea what tactic to employ. Swing, furiously; our seemingly only defense against this speeding bullet. Use our measly strength to counter what bombards us, which seems slight compared to what screams of MAJOR. Stand frozen and afraid, HOPING we will not be hit by the onslaught of such a powerful strike. Or worse, turn in our tracks, assuming we are a fake. We are unsuitable for this role we are playing, certainly a square peg in this round hole of life we are trying to conform to.

For me CONFORMITY, I realized, worked for sixty years, UNTIL IT DIDN'T! I became very adept at playing the game of LIFE. I dislike playing games, by the way, games of all kinds. Board games, card games, and most certainly the mind games some like to play deplete me. My goodness, those are the absolute worst. If I play a card game with my family, the part where we all lay our cards on the table, we all know what we have…no more secrets, no more holding back; this for me is the most FREEING. If there is a secret to be held; only the 'HAPPY' kind, please! My son is coming home from deployment and surprising me after a years-long absence. My daughters are all hiding the fact that their dad is surprising me with a diamond necklace, the sex of a long-awaited grandbaby upon birth; these are the 'SECRETS' of life that I can have kept from me.

But dark secrets have no place for me any longer. My secrets that I have kept for half of a century have led me down many a dark corridor. Suppressed memories from a dissociative spotty childhood helped me survive, *but surviving is NOT THRIVING in God's Kingdom.* Journaling my years of recovered memories and trudging through yet more years of understanding and healing led to much insight.

What I have learned from re-experiencing my trauma through the feelings and emotions of EMDR[1] during therapy: *Our body remembers even when our mind refuses.* We desire to force these memories to be hidden, not just from others but from ourselves as well. Our minds dissociate to help us do precisely that; we will dissociate from what is so dreadful that we cannot process. In doing so, much is held in our bodies that must be released. It was a cataclysmic occurrence that left me reeling for the better part of three years. But our bodies must RELEASE THIS if healing is to occur. Our minds must accept what our body tells us happened if we accept this walk that the Lord has for us; our authentic and genuine healing through HIM.

Healing is a tall order for those messed with and messed up by abuse, neglect, or hurt from this fallen world. Many a scar remains. But as is God's way, these challenges are opportunities to grow in the *amount of honesty with which we can accept.* Trust me when I say that there were many times I found myself taking the two steps forward only to retreat the same two steps back, it would seem. *Discovering horrific, forgotten, or dissociated memories IS TRAUMATIC IN ITSELF.* As healing continues much growth and insight are gained. We come to the realization that we have lived much of our lives out of our wounds of the past. When we finally reach the end of ourselves, life certainly takes on new brilliance and depth. Through much hard work, shedding layers in the hands of Our Healer leads to eventual peace. MERCY and GRACE imparted on us by this Sovereign God need only be accepted out of FAITH, TRUSTING IN THE TRUTH OF HIS WORD.

I stand as living proof that being 'BRAVE' ENOUGH, or 'SMART' ENOUGH, or even 'BRIMMING' WITH FAITH is not a prerequisite to healing childhood trauma or profound, to the core, soul wounds. What it does take is HOPE IN OUR LIVING GOD. TRUST that even our 'mustard size' FAITH will move the mountain of pain we lay at JESUS' FEET AS WE COME TO HIM DAILY praying for healing and health. I've felt the COURAGE come, I've learned from the SCRIPTURES, He's led me to, and I've seen my FAITH increase with each passing month. From the root of my pain to the core of my wounds, God has shown me that I am enough, I am healing, and I am more than enough for this battle that I am fighting.

---

[1] EMDR or Eye Movement Desensitization and Reprocessing Therapy: This procedure incorporates bilateral sensory stimulation while focusing on the trauma memory. The vividness and EMOTION of the memory or physical sensations are reduced over time as traumatic experiences are integrated into "normal" memories associated with the past.

Healing is a tall order for those messed with and messed up by abuse, neglect, or hurt from this fallen world. Many a scar remains. But as is God's way, these challenges are opportunities to grow in the amount of honesty with which we can accept.

Trust in the Truth of His Words.

CONTENTS

An Encounter Of
Epic Proportions

It has been one of life's mysteries to me, as I have looked over my life, the sweetly remembered memories filed away as if to be treasured and held close. Beautiful thoughts that hold special or significant meaning in the design of one's life. One such memory is cataloged in my heart as my first true encounter with Jesus. If I close my eyes, I can still see Him nestled between His mother Mary, and His stepfather, Joseph. The picture is so clear, perfectly painted as if it was a snapshot in time, placed ever-so-carefully on the bluest blue scrapbook of Jesus' ancestry and life story…also known as THE BIBLE, with pictures. I could not have been more than eight years old when I checked this book out from our tiny library in the obscure town in which I lived. This, along with 'Pipi Longstocking'. Pipi, a young adolescent, found herself shipwrecked on an island, haphazardly babysitting very young children and babies, and it did draw my attention away from this Bible a bit… Hey, I was only 8! But I fell in love with Jesus and His beautiful family. I was mesmerized by the pictures, and I yearned to know more. As I searched those shelves later that summer, there seemed no trace of the magnificent blue book I so longed to retrieve; there was so much more I felt I needed to know about this Jesus.

And here I am, 55 years later, with my own Blue Bible, the pictures drawn by ME, emphasizing much that needs retaining. I, like Pipi, have haphazardly, at times, raised my 8 children. I have somewhat let that draw my attention away from my bible, but not my love for Jesus. As my children have moved into their own lives, more time is left to explore. To explore who we are as a couple; my husband, Geno, and me. A full house and busy schedules certainly allowed little time for that over the years. Try as we might, 'best-laid plans' for time away from our children seemed to become next year's vacation WITH THE CHILDREN, showing them all the 'fun', they missed out on. Hence, we ALWAYS traveled with our littles…and we had A LOT OF LITTLES. It seemed easier, we decided, to let them have adventures alongside us.

Now was the time to venture out on our own, explore, enjoy, and live the carefree life of 'empty nesters'. Best-laid plans, for us, are NEVER easily obtained. My husband, Geno, and I spent the early years, instead tirelessly working together to tackle 'the MUCH' that was thrown our way.

I learned within this time, that just as our memories file away those treasured 'beautiful thoughts' and more importantly, FEELINGS toward something OR SOMEONE; our minds just as readily file away the 'horrific and the awful', the feelings toward something or someone. The memories get *'locked away'* inside our minds and our bodies until EVENTUALLY, THEY manifest themselves in different ways.

I think it helps to compare the healing of physical trauma to psychological trauma. Understanding that in both instances real damage from the effects of the trauma needs to be addressed and managed in a way that healing can occur, and life can be lived as normally as possible.

In an accident, let's say, that involves a physical injury to your leg; consequently, walking is difficult or impossible. This injury would likely take you to your doctor's office. After examining you, the doctor discovers much swelling and is alerted to a bigger problem, a possible broken bone. You are sent to receive an x-ray, and then to wait for the swelling to subside. Following all of this, finally, a cast or a splint is placed on your leg. After 6-8 weeks, the cast is removed, only to discover that now you require hours of physical therapy to help get this leg to work as it had worked in the past. This will take yet another 6 weeks, as well as much hard work on your part. To your frustration, a small slip from the ladder while hanging those curtains caused quite a ripple effect! This was A HUGE PROCESS to achieve the adequate healing this body needed.

Now imagine you are driving home from work one fall evening. Someone plows towards you as they dodge to avoid a deer in the oncoming lane. Your instincts automatically kick in, pulling you to the safety of the shoulder of the road. But the car behind you is not so lucky, the head-on collision is immediate, and both cars are soon engulfed in flames. You feel helpless. Grabbing your phone, as you jump out of your car, you dial 911. You wait and watch frantically and helplessly at a distance, knowing you can do NOTHING to change this. You could not have prevented it, you were helpless in this circumstance, and you prayed to God to take back this horrific happening. You find yourself begging God not to have to see or experience it. Retelling it to the many firefighters, police, and ambulance drivers is terrible, YET must be done to let all that is horrid out of your body and mind, as well for the police records. For months, the dreams come, the screams of the victims… or are they yours, they intermingle…until you know you need help to calm the chaos in your mind. And THIS, you are told, is PTSD. Now to tackle the healing.

A broken leg is seen, externally, on an X-ray, and it is seen by others, as one is in a cast and hobbling on crutches. Sympathy is given by all; who wouldn't be EMPATHETIC and open the door for someone with crutches, struggling to fit in the semi-opened door? Of course, we would. But what about THAT someone, YOU? YOU saw that terrible accident, YOU see that every night when you close your eyes. YOU hear those screams, were they screaming in those cars, could YOU have changed what happened? Was it your FAULT? Why don't they see YOU? Do they NOT SEE the pain of YOU reliving these moments over and over again? Why do YOU feel so invisible when you are fighting through PTSD? Yup, that was me asking those questions, or ones very similar to those for quite some time.

Yet for me, finding out that I suffered from C-PTSD[2] seemed to answer many questions in my mind as to my behavior; it was actually a bit freeing. You see, I spent much of my life in uneasiness and fear. Oh, I was great at covering it with busyness; 'FAKE IT TILL YOU MAKE IT' was my mantra for many years.

I was the girl in High school who missed lots of school. I was the girl who seemed fine… until I wasn't. I was the girl who felt completely different than everyone else. I think it's the feeling one gets when much school is missed; similar to showing up late to a party. The conversations are all underway, the groups are already formed; I walked in to be the girl on the outside looking in. I seem to understand the kids of today, who look for new titles and form different, unique groups…we all just want a place to fit in. Oh, how I wished I could have formed my OWN GROUP. But therein would have existed the problem. WHO was I? I arrived home from a Band Bus Trip without a clue why I was suddenly so VERY DIFFERENT. I rode a bus home in panic and fear, remembering only being given pills from a nurse sponsor to calm me. I remember a soft-spoken boy with glasses who looked over his seat from behind me in concern. I am sure, wondering where the excited,

---

[2] C-PTSD: Complex Post Traumatic Stress Syndrome involves trauma that is usually long-lasting trauma, not a one-time event as with PTSD, and typically the result of childhood trauma. This can cause flashbacks, nightmares, and insomnia, similar to PTSD, usually a bit more severe. The dreadful responses due to the effects of the TRAUMA: repressed memories, disconnecting from themselves, feeling hopeless, suicidal thoughts, depression, and viewing oneself as completely different than those around them, just to name a few.

happy-go-lucky snippet of a little 9th grader had gone. Little did we all know she had left her body and would not show up for quite some time.

Sleepless nights, fear, and more fear enveloped me for the rest of the school year. My grades lagged through the rest of high school. Playing the flute in Band Class, I suddenly held this foreign instrument, without a clue that I was once proficient in reading notes. Facts, dates, and all things to be memorized could not be cataloged in my brain. As the years continued, I've come to decide, that one just GETS TIRED, ONE SLEEPS, I believe that was me. I did not know why I was afraid of sleep, why I feared the darkness, or why the school I was forced to return to sent me into a panic.

WELL, I did not know until much later. These were the memories that I had held hidden for the better part of my life. But why would I not? These frightful memories are truly ones that nightmares were made of; MY nightmares were made of. What we cannot face, we dissociate from, and I found, amazingly enough, I was able to suppress these abhorrent acts…until I couldn't. Until they started creeping out in scary and confusing ways. Ways in which therapy became my only option to find answers to big questions. After years of intense therapy, I have made sense of the mystery of my life.

LOCK IT DOWN ...

Find the good
life is beautiful
YOU ARE LOVELY
Rejoice in the Lord!
Trust in the LORD.

Just as our minds file away those treasured 'beautiful thoughts' and feelings; our minds just as readily file away the 'horrific and awful.

Trauma can remain 'locked away' inside our minds and body, and must be released if healing is to be obtained.

Healing...
Writing a new **Story.**

My return to journaling in correlation to TRAUMA therapy led to much discovery. EMDR and BRAINSPOTTING[3] launched me, unfortunately, into a most repulsive way to further discover traumas in my life, somatically[4] feeling the pain of the trauma inflicted. It seemed my mind wanted to take me back to the beginning. Fear of my dad's anger and violent outbursts which had been passed to him from his abusive father. Understanding this to be generational as he would recount stories to us near his passing, did little to alleviate the fear and damage to 6 young children who experienced it firsthand.

Remembered, uncomfortable nasty touching by my grandpa, as an 11-year-old; processed, and led to somatic feelings of nightly assaults by this man. As processing continued, my question was answered as to why I was never rescued by my grandma: she thankfully protected my 5-year-old sister in bed with her, but in turn, left me to fend for myself. The abandonment felt that long week, my sister and I were left with these grandparents, taught me the need to dissociate my body and mind from the terror and pain. As unhealthy as this sounds, I have come to accept what the experts believe; this is a way our minds cope with extremely stressful situations, and *it protects us from the full impact of the traumatic experience.*

As trauma therapy progressed and new dreadful feelings of hands grabbing at me alerted me to new, frightful memories; I truly spent many weeks in denial. I think part of me could not believe there was more…more trauma, more violence. But as processing continued, the

---

[3] BRAINSPOTTING is a "trauma-informed therapy" similar to EMDR. Whereas EMDR utilizes eye movements as a form of bilateral stimulation, brainspotting focuses the eye on a fixed gaze position. The position of your eyes, or where your gaze is directed, can unlock some deeper insights and connect with the emotion centers of the brain that have not yet been recognized. Therapists are specially trained in both EMDR as well as BRAIN SPOTTING. (Matt Gallagher, Med, LCPC)

[4] Somatic Experiencing: "To help address the ways traumatic stress disrupts the functioning of our nervous system. The felt sense is where the implicit memory lives and this is often a suitable path for walking the nervous system back to regulation." Devin Coogan March 22, 2022, https://www.simplepractice.com) After being through something horrific or painful, being in our body can be challenging. Many times we need to actively re-learn how to feel sensations in the body, to feel SAFE in the body we occupy. This Therapy (Somatic Psychotherapy)—a body-centered approach to healing, is a powerful exercise for recovering from PTSD because it counters both dissociation and hypervigilance. It is guided by the belief that our body holds our unprocessed emotions and traumatic experiences. Caution must be exercised as trauma is rediscovered, awareness during this process of neutral or positive empathetic connection to self must be established, a deficiency in this area can be re-traumatizing…(My memories came like a tornado, unfortunately, BEFORE this was established.) Much information can be gleaned about this type of therapy from Peter Lavine, Ph.D., referencing 'felt sensations'. His many books include WAKING THE TIGER, HEALING TRAUMA, SEXUAL HEALING, *Transforming the Sacred Wound*, and many more; all exploring and applying his expertise.

realization was that those hands were the hands of boys on a mission. Hands that dragged an innocent girl to a room to take what they wanted; to take what was not theirs. That girl was me, who part-way through this harrowing nightmare manifested my grandpa. Suddenly, a chilling, overwhelming experience became more than my psyche could handle. Dissociating from this savage sinister experience was my only escape. A rare type of amnesia called dissociative amnesia[5] stems from emotional shock or trauma and can result from being the victim of a violent crime or experiencing other trauma. I tend to believe, this is the VIOLENT CRIME OR OTHER TRAUMA one would talk of…and certainly, I felt this is where that little girl had left her body.

As my therapist, Matt, and I as well, had assumed, the trip had triggered memories of my grandpa's violent acts, now we were armed with the full extent of the damage. The damage done that day to a 14-year-old girl was too much for my mind to handle. Even as a 60-year-old woman, God graciously allowed the memories time to 'settle' before I was allowed time to experience a new memory. As much as I wanted to RUSH therapy, just get through all the dreadfulness that was constantly emerging, I was thankful God was gracious to me. He allowed healing between 'NEW' old memories. Time for me to build up my resilience after each breaking down of my spirit with the pain and sadness of it all.

Ecclesiastes 3:1 (ESV) For everything there is a season, a time for every matter under heaven:

Ecclesiastes 3:3 (ESV) a time to kill, and a time to heal; a time to break down, and a time to build up…

As I followed through in this Chapter in the Book of Ecclesiastes 3:8 (ESV) …a time to love, and a time to hate; a time to war, and a time for peace. I noticed this was how my emotions fluctuated as I processed all the yuck that I dug from my past. I fought myself much of the time. I left God out of the equation plenty. I struggled through, in my strength more times than I can count. Even when I thought I had come to the end of myself, I found, that unless

---

[5] Dissociative Amnesia: Gaps of memory, gaps or periods where someone cannot remember information about their life, or events in their past, they may forget a learned talent or skill. These voids in memory are more severe than normal forgetfulness and are not the result of another medical condition. Some people find themselves, in a strange place without knowing how they got there; traveled there on purpose, or wandered in a confused state. These blank episodes may last minutes hours, or days, and in rare cases, they can last for months or years. https://www.nhs.uk https://www.mayoclinic.org

we continue to learn and grow in and through Jesus, we are NOT at the end of ourselves. There is always more to this SANCTIFICATION process, and it is, I found out, a beautiful process when compared to the alternative. See, for me, there were plenty of times during my life, as well as many times during my fight to find the little girl, JULIE, that I wanted to give up on life. Satan whispers to us that we, as well as those around us, would be better off if that is what we chose. But God was always whispering of the 'BETTER' THAT WAS COMING: THE TIME FOR PEACE.

For me, putting out my JOURNALING in book form, *(LAID BARE)*[6], of my journey through my trauma was my way of releasing my pain. A releasing to all that needed; young and old, proof, that dreadful, horrific happenings can be fought through, in Our Father's strength. The fight is real, it is hard, and UNFORTUNATELY, the fight is DAILY. Our emotions and feelings can make us reel and rant and fall over and frustratingly over and over again as we heal from traumatic events of life. For me, the feelings needed to be authentic and oh-so-personal. Why? Because that is what I needed and wanted when I struggled through my feelings, emotions, pain, and hurt. My last book was too 'REAL' for some. Those were the people who did not need what the words cried out; those same words others NEEDED to hear…that silently ACHED to hear, "I AM NOT ALONE IN MY SUFFERING."

1 Thessalonians 4:18 (ESV) Therefore encourage one another with these words.

2 Corinthians 1:3,4 (ESV) Blessed be the God and Father of our Lord Jesus Christ, the Father of mercies and the God of all comfort, who comforts us in all our affliction, so that we may be able to comfort those who are in any affliction, with the comfort with which we are ourselves are comforted by God.

Romans 15:4 (ESV) For whatever was written in former days was written for our instruction, that through endurance and through encouragement of the Scriptures, we might have hope.

As I have walked further down my road to health and recovery, more freedom is felt. It is lovely to experience insights gained from much soul searching, therapy, and most importantly, time spent with the lover of my soul, My God and Savior. Peace has come,

---

[6] "Laid Bare: The Journey to Recovering the Wounded Child Within" is available on Amazon as well as the companion book "I am Worthy" journal/coloring book

MOSTLY, (we do live in a fallen world), and I can certainly see the beauty that surrounds me more readily than feel the heaviness of the violence which I know this world holds. I try to live each day searching for the good in all things and all people. It seems I have not been able to contain myself, as I, with all modesty, but with a bit of insight gleaned might share what I have learned through my PROCESS OF HEALING TRAUMA.

My process through the darkness has left its mark. It has humbled me, as well as pushed me beyond my comfort zone. But I have realized, through God, that all things are truly possible. When we set out to do a GOOD thing and we work through and with God, we accomplish much more than we could ever hope for, and my hope remains strong.

"Have I not commanded you? Be strong and courageous. Do not be frightened, and do not be dismayed, for the Lord your God is with you wherever you go." Joshua 1:9

FOR *everything* THERE IS A *time*

ECCLESIASTES 3:1

...a time to break down...
...a time to weep...

...a time to build up...

...a time to laugh...

...a time to seek...

...a time cast away...

...And a time for peace...

ENCOUNTER: REFINING GOLD

Meeting God in the healing

GOD TAKES US ON WINDING ROADS. WE KNOW NOT HIS WAYS: WHAT AN UNDERSTATEMENT. I found myself teaching sewing classes to a group of students who might call themselves misfits. I, a misfit myself and certainly not a teacher in the conventional sense of the word, fit right in. This school is one for kids struggling to graduate from traditional High Schools. Some, their 'last ditch' effort to receive a diploma before sending them out into the cold, cruel world. A world where they may well be accustomed to its cruelness, in ways the students left at previous schools might be UNAWARE. Those that don't live THAT life, where *monsters* might face them around every corner at home, or yelling is commonplace, or abuse is a way of life; cars might well BE these kids' houses, or food and money are hard to come by and makes school just another hurdle to overcome. Asking the question at times, "Why does life have to be so HARD?"

And why DOES life have to be SO HARD? Over the last few years, I've learned to ask God the HARD questions I wrestle with. In turn, He has delivered many HARD TRUTHS. But I bear in mind that God wants freedom for us. Remembering, as my children grew, their questions also grew with them. The easily answered, quickly turned to solar system trivia and abruptly accelerated to complex chemistry, which was swiftly passed off to my analytical husband. Frankly, the questions took thought/and or investigation. In the end, bigger, harder questions show growth and maturity in our children. Just as with the years of therapy I endured to come to the place of healing and growth from my trauma rediscovered, I also tended to ask more serious and complicated questions. God will give us answers, all we need to do is ASK the questions. (Matthew 7:7,8 (ESV) "Ask and it will be given to you, seek and you will find; knock, and it will be opened to you. For anyone who asks receives, and the one who seeks, finds, and to the one who knocks it will be opened.") I believe He doesn't want us sitting in the dark. Like any GOOD PARENT, He helps us on our way, even with the most difficult questions of our lives. Genesis 5:20 (ESV) You intended to harm me, but God intended it for good to accomplish what is now being done, the saving of many lives. Here, the 'saving of many' is possibly just the saving of ME! God opened a new door with every question I asked, even with curiosity that besieged me. This is not to say that many open doors and windows were not breezy, and at times slammed closed until my psyche was ready to handle all that blew in. Thankfully, God knows, THE TRUTH DOES, INDEED, SET US FREE. (2 Corinthians 3:17 (ESV) "Now, the Lord is the Spirit, and where the Spirit of the Lord is, there is freedom.")

Ironically, *freedom looks different to me now*. Sometimes we get so caught up in the BIG PICTURE of life, that we tend to move at a merciless pace. We, with our schedule of goals, our fixes, and our missions. Do we at times forget the small triumphs along the way, so concerned about the huge victory waiting for us at the finish line? For me, that finish line was 'COMPLETE' and total healing of all that held me bound from my past. Now wasn't that silly? Nonetheless, I confess it was. God wants freedom for us; of this, I am sure. (John 8:32 (ESV) "And you will know the truth, and the truth will set you free.") I believe that once I became a healthier version of myself, I started slowing down to notice the smaller wins in my life, and more importantly, from whom those wins came. 2 Corinthians 10:17 (ESV) "Let the one who boasts, boast in the Lord."

I'm learning through my journey, just how painful uncovering old trauma, as well as untapped soul wounds can be. Healing for me was a long, hard, arduous fight for freedom. No one truly knows what another faces, be gentle, have tolerance, and be kind, especially to YOURSELF. Be gentle as you manage your recovery; no one else carries the hidden wounds or the violence you endured. For me, everything about healing, 'somatically' remembered, seemed so foreign and strange. I was my harshest taskmaster, as I pushed and hurried my recovery. But healing all that our bodies experienced and stored, for however long, needs this period to repair. It should not be rushed. This goes for, not only your body but your mind, your Spirit, as well your soul. For me, this was not realized until years into my recovery. God finally teaching me that to be whole, 'NORMAL', healed of any signs of sexual abuse, and 'HAPPY' for all to see, was something akin to the world's view of SUCCESS. What God WANTS for us is to NOT be conformed to the world's views, but a deeper joy and peace; to live a satisfied life in HIM. (Romans 12:2 (ESV) Do not be conformed to this world, but be transformed by the renewal of your mind, that by testing you may discern what is the will of God, what is good and acceptable and perfect.)

This means a constant reminder of who we are in Christ. The labels that were pasted on us by others or ourselves need NOT be carried for a lifetime. Much time is needed as this renewal of our mind takes place. I realized this is where science collided with all that I was learning in therapy and scripture about renewing my mind. In my years of marinating in the negative aspects of unworthiness, the mantle worn by me from my childhood abuse felt heavy. When I realized this was something I could 'heal' by replacing this and other negative thoughts with scripture, affirming God's truth of the matter, was life-giving. I dug in my heels; truly GOD'S OPINION is the ONLY opinion that matters.

Isaiah 43:4 (ESV) Because you are precious in my eyes and honored, and I love you.

Psalm 46:5 (ESV) God is in the midst of her; she shall not be moved; God will help her when morning dawns.

John 15:9 (ESV) As the Father has loved me, so I have loved you. Abide in my love.

Luke 12:6,7 (ESV) Are not five sparrows sold for two pennies? And not one of them is forgotten by God. Why, even the hairs on your head are all numbered. Fear not, you are of more value than many sparrows.

Deuteronomy 31:8 (ESV) It is the LORD that goes before you. He will be with you; He will not leave you or forsake you. Do not fear or be dismayed."

Zephaniah 3:17 (ESV) The LORD your God is in your midst, a mighty one who will save; He will rejoice over you with gladness; he will quiet you by his love; he will exult over you with loud singing.

Ephesians 2:10 (ESV) For we are His workmanship, created in Christ Jesus for good works, which God prepared beforehand, that we should walk in them.

I put my trust in God's word. I let myself marinate in HIS TRUTHS. As Pastor Craig Groeschel[7] preached, I used cognitive reframing, interpreting circumstances through the goodness of God. A God who is ALWAYS faithful. A God who wants me whole, healed, and serving Him in the plans HE HAS FOR ME and in which HE HAD in the BEGINNING. I constantly affirmed, through scripture, TRUTH, negating those lies

---

[7] Pastor Craig Groeschel's sermons.love https://sermons.love > craig-groeschel cognitive reframing/interpreting your circumstances based on the truth of God's word.

spoken or implied to me and over me as a child. It is when we understand that God has our life's purpose laid out for us, what others see as my 'TOO MUCH', God and I see as our GREATEST STRENGTH NEEDED FOR OUR BATTLE. My life changed when I finally REALIZED MY VALUE AND accepted my value IN CHRIST. The true freedom in Jesus Christ was being revealed. I was suddenly learning to love the little girl, me, in her vulnerability, not despise her for not fighting harder, and accept that I could NOT STOP WHAT WAS DONE TO ME as a child. I was able to appreciate the resilience of my character. For the first time, I was able to see the GOODNESS in me, to see myself, NOT as a flawed being, who was dirty, or worse. The labels I'd worn, given by fingers pointed at me to draw attention away from guilty parties and point to someone unwilling to fight. YES, renewing our minds in God's strength is possible. Renewing the truth of who we are, through Jesus' sacrifice on the cross: A perfectly imperfect NEW creation through Jesus Christ who longs only to see the goodness in others, now that we have truly understood how far God has gone to show us the GOODNESS IN HIM.

SHEDDING LAYERS IN THE HANDS OF OUR HEALER
LEADS TO EVENTUAL PEACE, MERCY, AND GRACE
IMPARTED ON US BY THIS SOVEREIGN GOD NEED
ONLY BE ACCEPTED OUT OF FAITH, TRUSTING IN
THE TRUTH OF HIS WORDS.

"Now the Lord is the Spirit, and where the Spirit of the
Lord is, there is freedom." 2 Corinthians 3:17

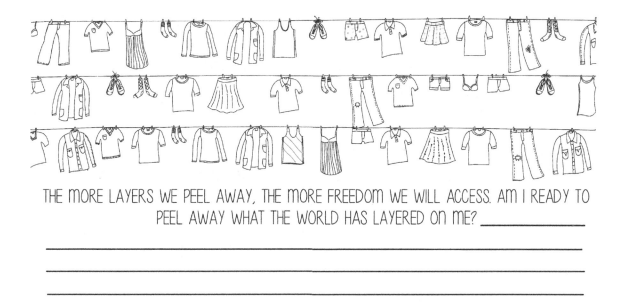

THE MORE LAYERS WE PEEL AWAY, THE MORE FREEDOM WE WILL ACCESS. AM I READY TO
PEEL AWAY WHAT THE WORLD HAS LAYERED ON ME? _____

_____

_____

_____

LORD, help me to see what layers I need released in my life to lead a more authentic life in YOU. As I reflect on this, guide me to where I can begin my healing journey...

_____
_____
_____
_____
_____
_____
_____
_____
_____
_____
_____
_____
_____
_____
_____
_____
_____

Out of my distress I called on the LORD; the LORD answered me and set me free.

Psalms 118:5

For freedom Christ has set us free; stand firm therefore, and do not submit again to a yoke of slavery.

Galatians 5:1

As the Father has loved me, so I have loved you. Abide in my love. John 15:9

God is in the midst of her; she shall not be moved; God will help her when morning dawns. Psalm 46:5

God's Truth

The LORD your God is in your midst, a mighty one who will save; He will quiet you by His love; He will exult over you with loud singing. Zephaniah 3:17

Because you are precious in my eyes and honored, and I love you. Isaiah 43:4?

"It is the LORD that goes before you. He will be with you; He will not leave you or forsake you. Do not fear or be dismayed." Deuteronomy 31:8

Deep Calls To Deep

Go deeper, you won't drown!

I WONDER AT TIMES IF GOD'S PERFECT LOVE IS AN ATTRIBUTE THAT IS SO FAR OUT OF our realm of understanding we struggle at times to accept it. This is, perhaps, the only 'why' or 'how' I have been reluctant, in the past, to surrender my life wholeheartedly to my Maker. Why I continually, in my human weakness, would forge through, plowing against impossible odds, in my strength, to no avail. Then, when I'd hit the wall, what else was there to do, ah, yes to pray? Why is that a last resort for many as opposed to our first line of action in this world of many trials? I doubted God's love for me. I was listening to the lie of my childhood, "God is too busy for the likes of ME; He has more important things to do." And, unfortunately, believing those lies on a deep internal level without even realizing this; I had never addressed the lie.

But the beauty of the Holy Spirit living inside us, with inner groanings, sometimes deeper than words, we are enlightened to what God is speaking to us; where we have room for change…OR telling us, HE JUST FLAT-OUT LOVES US, JUST BECAUSE HE LOVES US. His arms are always holding us. Gone are the days I believed, 'It's only on the other side of death that I get to curl into the safety, security, and never-abusive hands of this ever-loving God.' It is a deep and sincere longing to seek unity with our God who made us. HE IS MY 'DEEP THAT CALLS TO DEEP'. (Psalm 42:7 (ESV) Deep calls to deep in the roar of your waterfalls; all your waves and breakers have swept over me.) When in a place of despair, knowing all that God has done in my past and praying for the confidence to once again, praise Him in my present. When the deep trials of affliction want to sweep our legs out from under us, we need deep restoration. And in this world, WE WILL HAVE THESE TRIALS; thank goodness our God is BIGGER. James 1:12 (ESV) "Blessed is the man who remains steadfast under trial, for when he has stood the test he will receive the crown of life, which God has promised to those who love Him."

Romans 11:33 (ESV) Oh, the depth of the riches and wisdom and knowledge of God! How unsearchable are His judgments and how inscrutable His way! His greatness dwarfs my neediness in all my 'deep thinking, deep loving, and deep hurting'. He surpasses THIS by giving His Son to die for ME!

John 3:16 (ESV) "For God so loved the world, that He gave His only Son, that whoever believes in Him should not perish but have eternal life." DEEP TRULY CALLS TO DEEP.

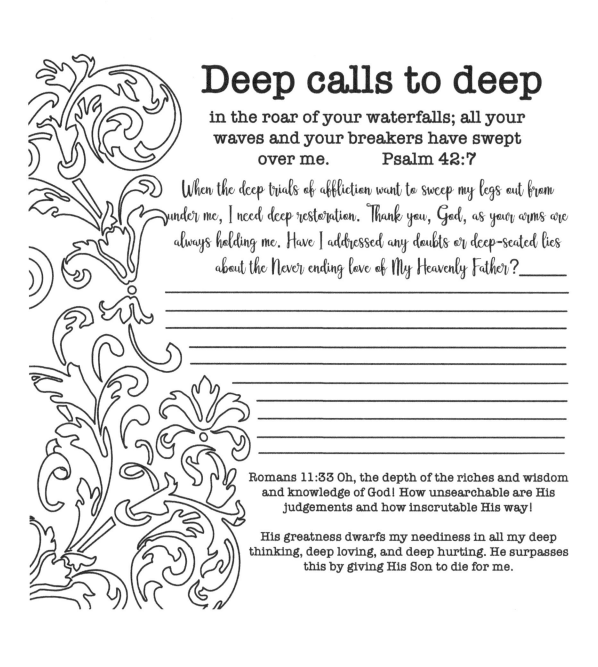

Deep calls to deep

in the roar of your waterfalls; all your
waves and your breakers have swept
over me.   Psalm 42:7

When the deep trials of affliction want to sweep my legs out from
under me, I need deep restoration. Thank you, God, as your arms are
always holding me. Have I addressed any doubts or deep-seated lies
about the Never ending love of My Heavenly Father?_____

_____
_____
_____
_____
_____
_____
_____
_____

Romans 11:33 Oh, the depth of the riches and wisdom
and knowledge of God! How unsearchable are His
judgements and how inscrutable His way!

His greatness dwarfs my neediness in all my deep
thinking, deep loving, and deep hurting. He surpasses
this by giving His Son to die for me.

RADICAL GRACE

His Grace flooded my wounded heart.

My profound realization of GRACE, I suppose, could be compared to another's conversion to Christianity. I was confused about why I could not, like all others in my Bible Study group, feel this LOVE of God I read about week after week, year after year. A God I believed in, loved, and wanted to worship. I did believe all that this Holy Bible talked of. I believed in all the miracles. I believed in the most wonderous, miraculous resurrection of God's Son, Jesus. But to say that God loved me, of all people; no, this seemed out of my realm of possibilities. I did not seem worthy of His love. Try as I might, the harder I forced scripture in, the more flawed and broken I felt. Now, I know, we are all sinners, saved by the death of God's ONE AND ONLY SON that He sent to our forever sin-stained world to cover that sin and set us free from all this condemnation. (Romans 8:1 (ESV) There is therefore now no condemnation for those who are in Christ Jesus.) I suppose, even back then, I certainly WAS NOT taking God at HIS WORD in all that He had done for me. But try as I might, I fell short in the belief of MY worthiness...UNTIL GRACE, ever so gently took my hand, led me to the MERCY that is JESUS, OUR SAVIOR. That Wednesday afternoon, I suddenly knew, Jesus would leave those ninety-nine sheep in search of me; I mattered to HIM.

In the years that followed, there was a new understanding of this undeserved MERCY. The open-handed receiving of God's mercy was undeserved but certainly praiseworthy. Peace seemed to settle in my Spirit as I learned how deep God's grace was for me. God's grace was so much kinder than the grace I would give myself over the next ten years of my life. As one looks at their life in retrospect, knowing the totality of truth, and the outcome of so many sleepless nights, how much gentler we would be on ourselves. Knowing now, how much strength the Psalms gave me as I read them, rewrote them, jotted notes and dates near them, made flourishes on them, as well as my fair share of doodles and artwork relating to many of them…did I get strength from them, as I assumed. Or, I wonder now, did God speak directly to me, did HE keep me alive in HIS STRENGTH? Those years, as I started my slow but steady descent into the upheaval of my childhood trauma. I tend to believe the latter, His strength not only kept me alive but pushed me, the many times I had no will to live. (Psalm 2:1 (ESV) Blessed are all who take refuge in Him. Psalm 3:3 (ESV) But You, O LORD, are a shield about me, my glory, and the lifter of my head. Psalm 4:1 (ESV) Answer me when I call, O God of my righteousness! You have given me relief when I was in distress. Be gracious to me and hear my prayer. Psalm 4:7 (ESV) You have put more joy in my heart than they have when their grain and wine abound. Psalm 5:2 (ESV) Give attention to the sound of my cry, my King and my God, for you do I pray. Psalm 5:3 (ESV) Oh Lord, in the morning you hear my voice; in the morning I prepare a sacrifice for you and watch. Psalm 5:11 (ESV) But let all who take refuge in you rejoice; let them ever sing for joy, and spread your protection over them, that those who love your name may exult in you. Psalm 5:12 (ESV) For you bless the righteous, O LORD; you cover him with favor as with a shield.) And THIS…but one page into the Psalms!

The CHAOS that overtakes someone who is recovering suppressed memories; breaking generational strongholds that have held a family bound for generations, is not only a fight of our mind but very much a fight with our families as well. Self-discovery is painful, as well as alienating from those confused by the changes seen. For family members living in the dark, where therapy and the use of boundaries are very intentional, this seems counterintuitive: Sharing 'family secrets' with strangers. *Instinctively broken people seem to want to break others.* This is where I learned to apply that 'GRACE' I had learned of, so many years before. God pushed me through what seemed impossible in my power, extending grace to those with no understanding of healing through therapy.

God helped me realize those BOUNDARIES I'd been learning about in therapy and were applying, benefitted me. It was never about TELLING others what they can or cannot do. Those boundaries were about letting people in our life, finally know, that we have learned through our trauma and therapy, what WE WILL AND WILL NOT accept any longer. I took cues from scriptures where Jesus used boundaries. John 2:24 (ESV) "But Jesus would not entrust Himself to them, for he knew all people…" As well in Matthew 16:23 (ESV) in a conversation with Peter, "Get behind me, Satan! You are a hindrance to me. For you are not setting your mind on the things of God, but on the things of man." God has a plan for ALL OF OUR LIVES, we know this from scripture. (Jeremiah 29:11 and 2 Timothy

1:9 ESV) Jesus needed those boundaries as HE WAS FOLLOWING HIS PURPOSE, the PATH GOD SENT HIM to earth to accomplish.

I was suddenly starting to see that God's purpose for my life was so much MORE than I had ever dreamt it could be. I lived most of my life believing I must make life comfortable for all that exists in the space surrounding me. Be it family or friends, church companions, neighbors, or even those in line at the grocery store around me. I was the righter of all wrongs. I felt, just as I did growing up, that it was up to me to come to everyone's aid. While this is a very righteous and noble cause, it affords us no PEACE. I have come to believe, there will always be dragons to slay…but some dragons will always breathe fire. No matter how much water or LOVE we pour on them, we seem to CONTINUALLY get burned. A hard lesson learned to all 'DRAGON SLAYERS': SAVE YOURSELF (and your salve) …shower your love and kindness on those who long to be hugged and shown unconditional love and acceptance. Life is SO FILLED with these SOULS, WANTING nothing more than to just be loved! We are called to be KIND, caring, compassionate, filled with mercy, and so much more, but I do not believe God wants us to be continually kicked and treated harshly as we work toward healing ourselves.

Accept this RADICAL GRACE WE ARE EXTENDED FROM GOD, and ever so importantly, EXTEND THAT GRACE TO OTHERS! God helped me realize there CAN BE PEACE with an apology that SIMPLY DOES NOT COME: That apology NEVER HELD MY HEALING. This radical grace leads to so much change in our lives, but ONLY if we release our past hurts, grievances, and way of living with dysfunction and defensiveness. Move into our new future with grace and humility. Don't fight what God has for our future. The decision for me was a very conscious choice to focus on thankfulness. A battle won with God. A battle won one moment at a time with word after word from God. This is where applying that scripture; we must soak ourselves in day after day is imperative. God's word seeps into our SPIRIT, it takes root. When faced with difficult trials in our life we can dig from that deep well of knowledge of the TRUTH which IS the LIVING WORD OF GOD: The WORD that is ALWAYS alive and relevant.

2 Corinthians 9:8 (ESV) And God is able to make all GRACE abound to you, so that having all sufficiency in all things at all times, you may abound in every good work.

For the law was given through Moses; GRACE and TRUTH came through Jesus Christ. John 1:17 (ESV)

As I accept God's Grace, freely given, how has this affected my healing?
Am I living in more thankfulness? Am I sharing my gifts more fully as I am
more fully filled? _____

_____
_____
_____
_____
_____
_____
_____
_____
_____
_____
_____
_____

And God is able to make all grace
abound to you, so that having all
sufficiency in all things at all
times, you may abound in every
good work.
2 Corinthians 9:8

For the law was given through
Moses; grace and truth came
through Jesus Christ.
John 1:17

Radical Grace
Fully
Filled

"Don't fight what God has for our future. Focus on thankfulness. The
battle is won one moment at a time with word after word from God.
Apply the scripture that you've soaked yourself in day after day. God's
word seeps into our Spirit, it takes root. When faced with trials, we dig
from this deep well of knowledge...THE LIVING WORD OF GOD." Julie

PEACEMAKING INDEED BRINGS PEACE

Be the Peace

"I have said these things to you, that in me you may have peace. In the world, you will have tribulation. But take heart; I have overcome the world." John 16:33 (ESV)

TRYING TO MAINTAIN THIS 'CONSTANT PEACE' CAN PROVE TRICKY. AS JOHN QUOTES Jesus... 'This world guarantees us tribulation'; taking HEART seems easier said than done. For those of us raised in 'PEACEKEEPER MODE', our instinct is to remain on 'high alert' to all that needs 'fixing' and 'attended to' to maintain the peace surrounding us. Quite frankly, this is exhausting when intergenerational trauma continually replicates itself or is HUSHED, NOT HEALED. Unhealthy methods of coping and interacting might be commonplace: Anger, passive-aggressive behavior, or total avoidance of distress and conflict. Whatever method of coping was used; children 'learn what they live' or is it 'cope and are colored by their abuse', and tend to avoid, at all costs, negative interactions.

For me, learning that *there is a vast difference between being a PEACEMAKER and a PEACEKEEPER* was transformational. Getting to the real issues and having honest, authentic conversations for genuine healing through PEACEMAKING is life-giving. Whereas PEACEKEEPING is draining and quite the opposite; getting to the core problem is NOT THE GOAL inasmuch as 'keeping all the balls in the air'. Much feels destructive, chaotic, uncertain, and certainly not live-giving; similar to the mayhem in which many of us may have survived our entire lives. I began to see this was how I operated, and it was truly overwhelming. It certainly was NOT how I (OR GOD) wanted to continue depleting my system. If we are to truly MAKE PEACE; to BE THE PEACE in this world, with the result of meeting others with GRACE; authentic, honest, candid conversations looking for sincere and genuine healing, we must be right-minded: MERCY-MINDED.

Micah 6:8 (ESV) He has told you, O man, what is good; and what does the LORD require of you but to do justice, and love kindness, and walk humbly with your God?

Luke 6:36 (ESV) Be merciful, just as your Father is merciful.

Am I a peacekeeper or a peacemaker? Differentiating the two is life altering. Quite possibly the contrast from chaos to calm in my life. Unlearning is hard. How can I start the process?

_____

_____

_____

_____

_____

_____

_____

"I have said these things to you, that in me you may have peace. In the world, you will have tribulation. But take heart; I have overcome the world. John 16:33

I AM A PEACEMAKER!

Be merciful, just as your Father is merciful.
Luke 6:36

FORGIVENESS DOESN'T ALWAYS MEAN RECONCILIATION

Choose to Shine

As I continually forge through this life, fighting to stay afloat at times; I do so, feeling BLESSED that God fights right alongside me through it all. When marriages fail, and let's be honest, sometimes they do. When brokenness occurs, unfortunately, we all experience this to a certain extent. When we lose that special someone or something that meant the world to us; when we think we cannot move forward from the pain and loss, and life seems to have gotten the better of us. These are times that can easily sink us, and maybe they do for a bit. Knowing who stays with us, in that pit, the entire time makes all the difference. "Do not be afraid or terrified because of them, for the LORD your God goes with you; He will never leave you nor forsake you." Deuteronomy 31:6 (ESV) (Isaiah 41:10 (ESV) Fear not, for I am with you; be not dismayed, for I am your God, I will strengthen you, I will help you, I will uphold you with my righteous right hand. Peter 5:7 (ESV) Casting all your anxieties on Him, because He cares for you. Jeremiah 29:11 (ESV) For I know the plans I have for you, declares the LORD, plans for welfare and not for evil, to give you a future and a hope.) GOD IS WITH US THROUGH IT ALL. PERIOD. These are words to hang onto; LIFELINES, when we feel the sorrows of loss, hurt, betrayal, and all the hard stuff life throws at us. He is near us when we are brokenhearted, and our spirits are crushed. (Psalm 34:18 ESV)

Jesus feels our pain; He guides us on our path as the sadness washes over us. Releasing my sorrow to God was quite a lengthy process; it was eventually replaced with hope. The journey to peace and joy could not be ushered in, for me, until the mourning subsided. Part of the process included *grieving my 'better past' that DID NOT EXIST*. Once realized, I could finally move toward the long road to acceptance and forgiveness.

Accepting deep hurts perpetrated against us, which seem not only UNACCEPTABLE but downright UNFORGIVABLE, is a process to be worked through. For some the anger is deep, for some like me, the anger turned inward to shame, and it seemed to know no limits. But we are called to forgiveness and so we must forgive. "Judge not, and you will not be judged; condemn not, and you will not be condemned; forgive, and you will be forgiven; give, and it will be given to you. Good measure, pressed down, shaken together, running over, will be put into your lap. For the measure you use, it will be measured back to you." Luke 6:37-38 (ESV)

Looking heavenward, knowing we are God's chosen ones, holy and beloved, (Colossians 3:12-14 ESV) we are to put on compassionate hearts, kindness, humility, meekness, and patience. We are to bear one another up, AND if one has a complaint against another, forgive each other; AS THE LORD HAS FORGIVEN YOU: SO, YOU MUST FORGIVE. And the ultimate part of this scripture…putting on LOVE WHICH BINDS EVERYTHING TOGETHER IN PERFECT HARMONY. God is the LOVE we crave, the compassion we have longed for. God is the kindness our hearts have searched for who LOVES us freely and unconditionally. Offering this to others in TRUE HUMILITY AND KINDNESS DOES BRING US HARMONY.

We must be willing to ACCEPT God's undeserved, unmerited, unearned forgiveness, which is forever, freely given. Only THEN are we free to forgive as God commands us; apart from GOD'S GRACE, we will always base our forgiveness on the offender's merit, worthiness, or remorse. MY ABILITY seemed to miss the mark on exactly how we forgive these major hurts in our lives and move forward. It is when we understand that the ABILITY to forgive those 'big hurts' comes from God, THROUGH the Holy Spirit living inside us, and MAKING ALL THINGS POSSIBLE! …OUR RESPONSIBILITY…once again, lifting our eyes heavenward, meeting our EVER-PRESENT FATHER who wants nothing more than to free us from the *self-imposed bondage* that unforgiveness holds us in. By FAITH, we lay our too-heavy weight before our Heavenly Father and TRUST HIM for restoration, TRUST HIM to be the perfect judge over the situation.

I felt somewhat euphoric as I threw forgiveness around like confetti. But truly the freedom felt was nothing short of miraculous…FOR ME… But here is where I realized forgiveness in relationships can be complicated. Not all come to this place of forgiveness at the same time. It is a process after all. Forgiveness starts with us and focuses on GOD, long before we can get to the point of looking to others. Some refuse to walk the hard walk of recovery; it is a tough path to walk with us. It is unhealthy and unfair to hold back our recovery based on their issues. *It takes two to RECONCILE, BUT FORGIVENESS can be a one-way street.* God calls us to, 'If possible, so far as it depends on you, live peaceably with all'. (Romans 12:18 (ESV) Reconciliation by definition: 'to be at peace again', should be the goal in healthy scenarios, but without God's supernatural work, ALONG WITH TWO PEOPLE apologizing, forgiving, compromising, and making changes, reconciliation is easier said than done. And let's be clear, sometimes those toxic people, once forgiven, need not hold space in our lives if we are to stay safe, healthy, and live in PEACE.

For HE HIMSELF is our peace, who has made us both one and has broken down in His flesh the dividing wall of hostility by abolishing the law of commandments expressed in ordinances, that He might create in Himself one new man in the place of two, so making peace, and might reconcile us both to God in one body through the cross, thereby killing the hostility. Ephesians 2:14-16 (ESV)

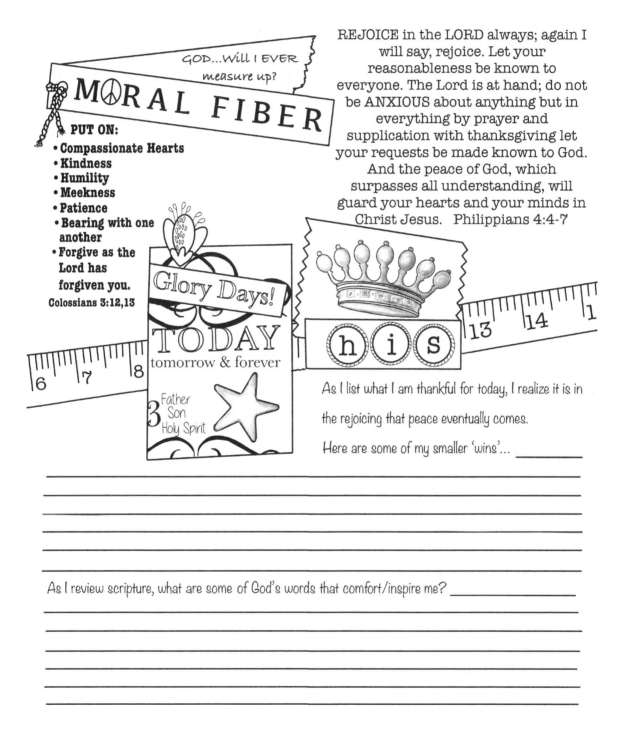

GOD...WILL I EVER measure up?

M☮RAL FIBER

PUT ON:
- Compassionate Hearts
- Kindness
- Humility
- Meekness
- Patience
- Bearing with one another
- Forgive as the Lord has forgiven you.

Colossians 3:12,13

Glory Days!
TODAY
tomorrow & forever

3 Father Son Holy Spirit

h i s

13 14

6 7 8

REJOICE in the LORD always; again I will say, rejoice. Let your reasonableness be known to everyone. The Lord is at hand; do not be ANXIOUS about anything but in everything by prayer and supplication with thanksgiving let your requests be made known to God. And the peace of God, which surpasses all understanding, will guard your hearts and your minds in Christ Jesus.   Philippians 4:4-7

As I list what I am thankful for today, I realize it is in the rejoicing that peace eventually comes.

Here are some of my smaller 'wins'... _____

_____
_____
_____
_____
_____

As I review scripture, what are some of God's words that comfort/inspire me? _____
_____
_____
_____
_____
_____
_____

Choose to shine

Releasing the sadness of my 'better past' takes time. I must always remember God is with the broken-hearted and crushed in spirit. Even when hurts seem "unforgivable"…I must forgive as I am called to forgive. It is a process! Lord, help me get started…

_____
_____
_____
_____
_____
_____

Lord, through the Holy Spirit, I thank You for perseverance in this process.

Take Courage/Trust

"Healing is the end of conflict within yourself." Stephanie Gailing

"BUT YOU, TAKE COURAGE! Do not let your hands be weak, for your work shall be rewarded." 2 Chronicles 15:7 (ESV)

BEING COURAGEOUS WAS COMPLICATED DURING THE YEARS OF DISCOVERY AND HEALING. Feeling the unworthiness that often accompanies child abuse victims, it is easy to forget that God is with us. I questioned my faith many times yet hung onto my trust in God's promises. We must constantly remind ourselves of what our Lord has done for us in the PAST, pushing us through to our hope for future restoration. Being in a desert, totally lost and alone, gives us much time for prayer and reflection. I found my years in the desert being 'tempted' to give up or give in to defeat were the most meaningful, prayerful years of my life. That is not to say, I would want to repeat time spent alone crying out for strength as well as breath in my lungs! I suppose it is true; 'it is not until we are lost that we find ourselves'. I'll go one step further and say…It is ADMITTING TO YOURSELF that you are utterly lost and alone and that without GOD'S guiding and healing hand can you truly BECOME found.

Reading the parable of the Prodigal Son, (Luke 15:11-24 ESV) I compared the image of his father to Our Heavenly Father. In the same way, Our Holy Father welcomes us with open arms as we fight His acceptance and His love, thinking we know better. (Luke 15:17 ESV) "But when HE CAME TO HIMSELF, he said, 'How many of my father's hired servants have more than enough bread, but I perish here with hunger! (Luke 15:19 ESV) I am no longer WORTHY to be called your son. Treat me as one of your hired servants. (Luke 15:20 ESV) And he rose and CAME TO HIS FATHER, but while he was still a long way off, HIS FATHER SAW HIM AND FELT COMPASSION, AND RAN AND EMBRACED HIM AND KISSED HIM."

Not only did this father, like OUR HEAVENLY FATHER, feel compassion and run to greet this prodigal, but he also clothed him in royal robes and celebrated his return. (Luke 15:24 ESV) 'For this son was dead, and is alive again; he was lost, and is found.' And they began to celebrate. We might feel like this wandering prodigal at times, lost in our past pain and our unworthiness. What a comfort to feel the embrace of Our Heavenly Father's Hug; knowing the security and peace for our soul rests in HIS LOVING PRESENCE.

Hebrews 11:1 (ESV) Now faith is the assurance of things hoped for, the conviction of things not seen.

Hebrews 11:6 (ESV) And without faith, it is impossible to please him, for whoever would draw near to God must believe that he exists and that he rewards those who seek him.

My soul seeks Him, and my faith remains strong as I continue to trust HIS HEALING.

Interrupt Anxiety With Gratitude

Be obsessively grateful.

"The secret of JOY is CHRIST in me—not me in a different set of circumstances." Elisabeth Elliot

Honestly, we ARE the ONLY ones who can control our thoughts. Though it feels like our mind, (literally), has a mind of its own. We swing from one scary thought to the next—one intrusive horrid memory to the last. Escaping the roller coaster of anxiety takes SERIOUS work. It is a conscious effort we must make, sometimes minute by minute to achieve this place of interruption of anxiety-free thinking. It is a constant reminder of letting God rule my life AND MY MIND: Giving God His rightful place of control.

Behold, You delight in the truth in the inward being, and You teach me wisdom in the secret heart. Psalm 51:6 (ESV) …And this translation (Psalm 51:6 Complete Jewish Bible) … Still, you want truth in the inner person; so, make me know wisdom in my inmost heart.

We must always keep in mind God's thoughts are encouraging, reassuring, calming, convicting, comforting, enlightening, and always leading us toward HIMSELF. It's when we forget who's driving our life and our headspace at times when things go south. Our thoughts overwhelm us with confusion, worry, condemnation, fear, and discouragement… they push and pull and rush at us until we are lost without hope UNLESS we force our thoughts on God, on His words, HIS HOPE. (Romans 15:13 (ESV) May the God of hope fill you with all joy and peace in believing so by the power of the Holy Spirit you may abound in HOPE. Philippians 4:6-7 (ESV) …do not be anxious about anything, but in everything by prayer and supplication with thanksgiving let your requests be made known to God. And the peace of God which surpasses all understanding will guard your hearts and your minds in Christ Jesus. 2 Timothy 1:7 (ESV) …for God gives us a spirit not of fear but of power and love and self-control. 1 John 4:18 There is no fear in love, but perfect love casts out fear. 1 Peter 5:7 (ESV) …casting all your anxieties on him, because He cares for you.) Even as I write the scriptures, do they sound trite? OR do I dig in deep? Do I take to HEART what is being said to me? MY GOD IS HOPE when I have felt hopeless. When I've been confused, God's Spirit promises me self-control (Some Bible versions word it…sound mind…EVEN BETTER!) The condemnation, discouragement, and anxiety can be fought WITH MERE WORDS. "IN EVERYTHING BY PRAYER AND THANKSGIVING!" And the peace of God, the likes of which we cannot even understand, will guard our hearts and our MINDS in Jesus Christ! And that fear that was crushing us, God promises HIS PERFECT LOVE CASTS OUT THAT FEAR. Here is when we turn our minds to God's perfect love for us. His UNENDING GRACE for us. His MERCY that is given. But more applicable, when negative thoughts rush, a positive for every one of those negatives. A BLESSING for every bad thought that might escape. The WORD: OUR SWORD for battle against the enemy. (Ephesians 6:17 ESV) This is when we continue to count our blessings given, all that we are thankful for. (Luke 6:45 ESV Her mouth speaks from that which fills her heart.) Fill ourselves FULLY with the OVER ABUNDANCE of God's BLESSINGS.

Living a life peacefully means living surrounded by positive, Spirit-filled people, content with who they are in the Lord. For me, this means listening to where the SPIRIT (sometimes Just a 'gut' feeling…*OR…is that the small still voice of the SPIRIT?*) leads me. Certainly, avoiding those who are not supportive, who live out of negativity, and who tend to lead conversations away from Our LORD'S WORD. I find that existing day-to-day with trust that the Lord will meet our needs. Knowing peace is tethered to God, not this world and its wily ways; listening to what HE wants for us, as opposed to our plan for the day. But of course, our humanity wants to jump in and take over much of the time. The learning curve is an ongoing process for all who are being sanctified (the process of being made holy, set apart for a special purpose) in this life. But always HOPE as Isaiah writes, "…fear not, for I am with you; be not dismayed; for I am your God; I will strengthen you, I will help you, I will uphold you with my righteous right hand." Isaiah 41:10 (ESV)

Take precious time out of your day to BE STILL WITH HIM. God is gracious to us; He wants this peace in our inward person. He has entered into this beautiful COVENANT LOVE with us; His love for us has no limits. He wants this growth we crave, this wisdom we long for, and this TRUTH THAT ALLOWS US FREEDOM from our past.

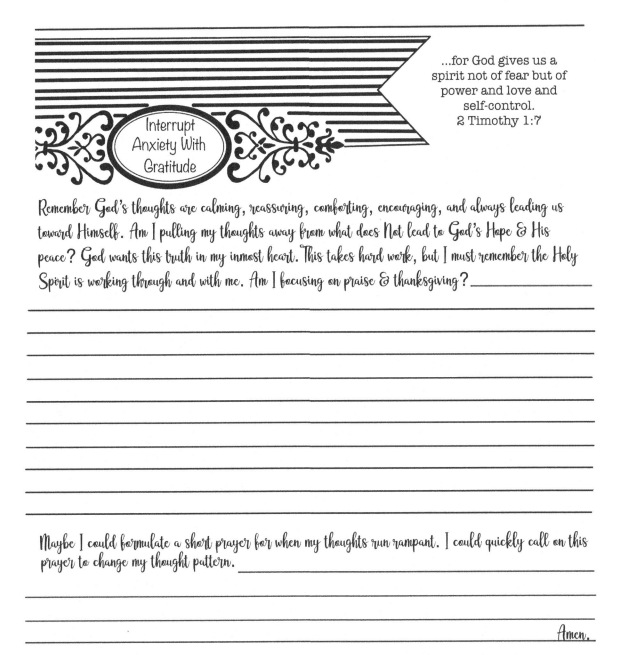

Interrupt Anxiety With Gratitude

...for God gives us a spirit not of fear but of power and love and self-control.
2 Timothy 1:7

Remember God's thoughts are calming, reassuring, comforting, encouraging, and always leading us toward Himself. Am I pulling my thoughts away from what does Not lead to God's Hope & His peace? God wants this truth in my inmost heart. This takes hard work, but I must remember the Holy Spirit is working through and with me. Am I focusing on praise & thanksgiving? _____

_____
_____
_____
_____
_____
_____
_____
_____
_____
_____

Maybe I could formulate a short prayer for when my thoughts run rampant. I could quickly call on this prayer to change my thought pattern. _____

_____
_____
_____ Amen.

...do not be anxious about anything, but in everything by prayer and supplication with thanksgiving let your requests be made known to God. And the peace of God which surpasses all understanding will guard your hearts and minds in Christ Jesus.
Philippians 4:6,7

SOUL-SUSTAINING SERVITUDE

We rise by lifting others.

"For you were called to freedom, brothers (and sisters). Only do not use your freedom as an opportunity for the flesh, but through love serve one another." Galatians 5:13 (ESV)

I FOUND THAT WHEN I WAS CAUGHT IN THE ROUGH WATERS OF LIFE. HELD BOUND BY whatever or whoever was speaking death into my soul, God would awaken within me an urgency to meet another's needs. If we look up, we can notice the ones around us who need our help. Wasn't that the theme of Christ's coming, all along: His ministry of giving, serving; culminating in sacrificing Himself to save ALL OF HUMANITY? I, fortunately, was called to serve, initially, in the softest and most pleasant of circumstances. As IS God's way; He is the gentlest of Fathers. As I healed my dreadful C-PTSD, nights so dreadful, my husband protected me from imagined past violators and abusers. I spent days exhausted and healing my body and mind. God sweetly put on my heart to sew for my 11 grandchildren, spending days with them when I felt healthy; loving, and more IMPORTANTLY, BLESSED BY THEM. Grandchildren are truly A GIFT FROM GOD, WORTH WAITING OUR LIFETIME FOR! These were times, so profound for me as I struggled to break the generational curse of rape by my grandpa and those before him. I love and want nothing more for these littles than freedom from this curse that had held our family for generations. But staying present in the present was a skill to be learned and acquired along the road to healing. This is not easy for those of us who must 'work through' our past trauma to find the healthy 'us' inside. Much needs to be fought through to get to that happier, healthier YOU. That 'you' that has been hiding scared, underneath all the layers that have shielded you from a dreadful past of abuse. But our children and grandchildren deserve the BEST of us. And I believe our inner child also deserves the best of us: A RESCUE from all that held her captive. The search to find the truth of secrets held, too frightening to face as a child, once recovered, sets us free to live the freedom of life in the present. "I will walk about in freedom, for I have sought out your precepts." Psalm 119:45 (ESV)

"Now the Lord is the Spirit, and where the Spirit of the Lord is, there is freedom." 2 Corinthians 3:17 (ESV)

"It is for freedom that Christ has set us free. Stand firm, then, and do not let yourselves be burdened again by the yoke of slavery." Galatians 5:1 (ESV)

I am working through my past to find the healthy me inside. Who would have known that breaking free from all that has been layered on me would bring more pain...

Healing is not an easy endeavor. What are some of my biggest challenges as I have fought for my peace and my freedom?

_____
_____
_____
_____
_____
_____
_____
_____
_____
_____

DISCOVER THE

LAYERS

IT'S TIME...
BREAKING FREE

They are Able because they think they are Able...
..virgil..

"I will walk about in freedom, for I have sought out your precepts."
Psalm 119:45

Family & Friends ...
... who stays?

TIME FOR...

MY

STORY

·····Still····Breathing·····

How have my family and friends received my story? _____
_____
_____
_____

Do I feel supported? _____
_____

GOD IS FOR US

Embrace your Holiness.

WE ARE CALLED TO *LIVE IN THE PRESENT*...IT IS A GIFT AFTER ALL! THIS IS POSSIBLY THE hardest lesson God taught and is still teaching me. For those of us who have been mistreated, misused, and abused, we tend to find ourselves doing one of two things, I believe. By no fault of our own, especially through the recovery period, we feel terrified, scrambling to survive; we feel 'undone' dealing with the fallout of therapy sessions, certainly NOT in control of our healing, our emotions, and to an extent, our bodies. Continually feeling undone by the 'phantom' pains, somatically felt, which are anything but invisible, and flashbacks of dreadful memories. So, living 'IN' THE PRESENT is frightening and even painful. A time to shrink and hide, duck, dodge, and dissociate as we have been doing for years to hide from all the dreadfulness that is our past.

On the flip side, living in the PRESENT during recovery, feeling like a fake. I was not sure who I was anymore. Sure, I knew I was a married woman, (until I forgot...) until night when I melted into a heap; a young girl being raped, reliving, unfortunately, all that was done to me as a preteen and teen. I lived a life in the 'in-between'. I felt I couldn't live in the present because I didn't FIT IN UNTIL I WAS FIXED. I started venturing out, as the 'FAKE HAPPY', I'M 'FINE' woman, an 'all but done' person, the gal who had survived a fiery trial of transformation; and written a book, nonetheless. But still lived, waiting for the magical day I was truly whole. Surrendering to God, a daily battle, certainly not the 'ONE AND DONE' deal I had come to believe in my first book. I realized as FEAR continued to haunt me; that I wasn't done yet. Asking God, the hard question about why fear persisted, led to more processing. Like a thunderbolt, God smacked me, assuring me, until death, hang on...YOU are never DONE being 'fixed', made whole...SANCTIFIED. Breathe in, breathe out, you ARE in the PRESENT, very much alive, and God is NOT DONE WITH ME YET! So, to those of us struggling to 'just get out of our heads', 'just live in the present' during our RECOVERY process, we say, "I am working on what is in my head, so that I CAN, just like everyone else, LIVE IN THE PRESENT, thank you very much." Many complex trauma survivors feel trapped in the past and would give anything to NEVER go there again. In talking about it, we finally find our way out of the maze of our past hurts. *It is only once we are out of the maze of discovery, hurt, and fear that I believe we can truly stay present.*

And for those of us who choose to unpack all that has held us bound: HOORAY FOR US! This will be the most beneficial and rewarding work you will ever do. It is hard, wearisome work. Even when feeling overwhelmed, afraid, lost, and forgotten by many; when we would like nothing more than to curl up and be done; this is when God's strength is working through us in powerful ways. For me, it was truly a fight for MY LIFE! (Psalm 105:4 (ESV) Seek the LORD and His strength; seek His presence continually!) The harder we try in our strength, the feeble and more fearful it all becomes. This freedom God wants; learning to release, to HIM, the darkness and injustice of this cruel world; not allowing it to squelch the light inside us… This is HUGE! For a sensitive soul to see and even feel a bit of the perversion in this fallen world is overwhelming. For me and my 'somatic ways', feeling evil, of but a snippet of a little girl's life (my exiled[8] little girl), when presented with it first-hand rocked me to my very core. With a discovery of this magnitude, I believe God gave me an insight into how evil this world can truly be. BUT THE GOOD NEWS, 'THE GOSPEL' is just that. As bad as it looks or 'FEELS' when presented with the weight of evil, GOD WINS. GOD'S LOVE WINS EVERY TIME! And that IS THE GOOD NEWS OF THE GOSPEL! But to be free from the darkness that threatened to drown me from the inside out is a POWER GOD WANTS FOR, not just me, but ALL OF US. Recovery is a choice—a HARD CHOICE, but a choice, nonetheless. God wants us to live in HIS GLORIOUS LIGHT! God is fighting for us and with us, ALWAYS!

---

[8] Exiled…This term* is referred to when applying IFS therapy: Internal Family Systems. This integrative approach to individual psychotherapy was developed by Richard Schwartz in the 1980s. It combines systems thinking with the view that the mind is made up of relatively discrete subpersonalities, each with its unique viewpoint and qualities. https://en.mwikipedia.org https://ifs-institute.com/about-us/richard-c-schwartz-phd.

* "Trauma can block our development in different parts of our psyche or identity creating an 'exile' that never feels accepted and reignites feelings of shame within us. This is (another) example where we might not find it adequate to simply use coping skills or cognitive/logical techniques since that is not the part of our brain reacting to our fears." Matthew Gallagher, Med, LCPC

The Gospel is this:
We are more sinful and
Flawed in ourselves than
We ever dared believe;
yet at the very same time
We are more loved and accepted in Jesus Christ
than we ever dared hope.

Timothy Keller

The reality is... I am not alone in my fight through
recovery; Jesus is fighting beside me. Jesus,
as my battle continues, I need to share all that
is on my heart today; unloading my burdens,
finding rest in You.

_____
_____
_____
_____
_____
_____
_____
_____
_____
_____
_____
_____
_____

CHILD-LIKE FAITH

If you are ready to grow....be ready to buy new clothes

I felt I lived this life of CHILD-LIKE existence for months on end as I rediscovered my childhood. For me living in God's 'GLORIOUS light' seemed like a constant fight. My fear of the DARK and all that I fought through at lights out, not to mention the darkness in me…add to that the oppression and violence of this fallen world tended to hold me bound. Living in this state of FEAR is certainly NOT how God would have us live. God wants freedom for us from our past that haunts us. *We are not called to live in VICTIMHOOD*: As always, 'scripture sheds light' on this…

In Matthew 18, the disciples are called to be humbled like children to enter heaven. But more than the 'Kingdom of Heaven'; to live in the 'here and now kingdom of heaven'… Jesus says, "Whoever receives one such child in my name receives me, but whoever causes one of these little ones who believe in me to sin, it would be better for him to have a great millstone fastened around his neck and to be dropped in the depth of the sea. Woe to the world for the temptation to sin! For it is necessary that temptation come, but woe to the one by whom the temptation comes!" (Matthew 18:5-7 ESV)

Jesus immediately follows this with words that SHOCK…of cutting off that which causes us to sin, be it a hand, a foot, or an eye. (Matthew 18: 8,9 ESV)

I tended to look at this scripture from a victim's standpoint until I referred to the setup of this scene. The disciples were asking Jesus, "Who is the greatest in the kingdom of heaven?" (Matthew 18:1 ESV) We MUST receive Jesus and HIS KINGDOM LIKE CHILDREN, HUMBLED, and MOST IMPORTANTLY, NOT CAUSING OTHER DICIPLES TO SIN. (Matthew 18: 3-6 ESV) Suddenly I was no longer the VICTIM of this scenario, I was a DISCIPLE of Jesus Christ with an OBLIGATION, as a follower, to heal my wounds. Heal by whatever means possible to live a life shining for Jesus' Kingdom, certainly not layering my YUCK on others, which only causes chaos and discord to those surrounding me. The sheer beauty of being a Christ follower; He meets us where we are in our journey. Yet being His follower, saved by His GRACE, increases our demand for accountability, it doesn't seem to allow us reckless excuses. 1 Peter 2:24 (ESV) He Himself bore our sins in His body on the tree, that we might die to sin and live in HIS righteousness. *BY HIS WOUNDS WE ARE HEALED*. And why would we waste our time on superficial worship when there is so much to be thankful for? Praise You, God, for our healing through Your Son, Jesus Christ.

He Himself bore our sins in His body on the tree, that we might die to sin and live in righteousness.

By His wounds you have been healed.
1 Peter 2:24

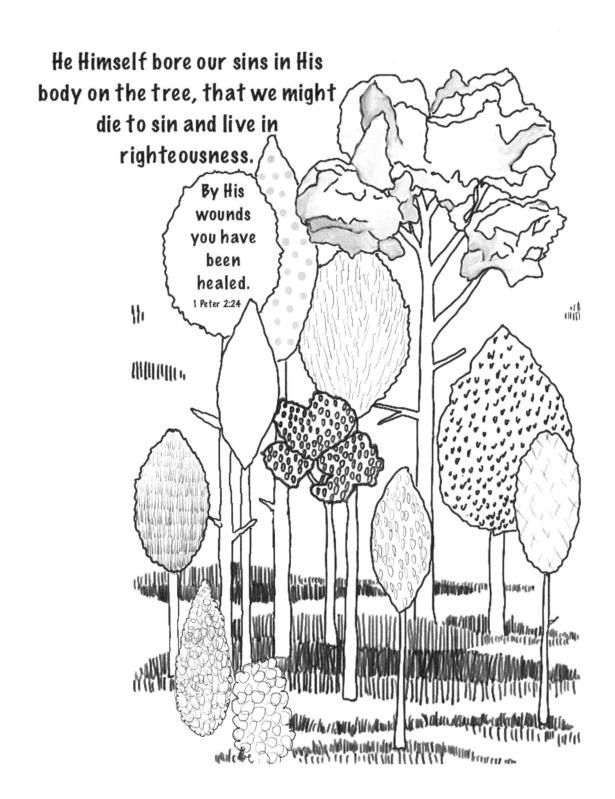

By His wounds we are healed.

I realize God doesn't want me living in fear, anymore than 'victimhood'.
What must I do alongside Christ to work toward healing my wounds?
He doesn't expect me to muscle my way out of my neediness,
but instead trust Him throughout this process.

_____

_____

_____

_____

_____

_____

_____

_____

_____

_____

_____

_____

_____

_____

_____

_____

Lord, I know that needing You is the key to knowing You more closely. Lord, help
me to focus on Your promises to guide me continually, even in scorched places.
(Isaiah 58:11)

WE SERVE A GENERATIONAL GOD

"You did not choose me, but I chose you." John 15:16 ESV

"JUST AS JESUS STEADFASTLY SET HIS FACE TO JERUSALEM, WE MUST STEADFASTLY GO UP to Jerusalem to fulfill God's purpose not our own." This quote by Tim Mackie of The Bible Project[9] rang true for me as I reflected on the deep sacred work of breaking generational strongholds.

DON'T LET THE LIES BE BIGGER THAN GOD'S TRUTH. That being said, for most of my life as it turned out, the lies loomed BIG, just as Satan would have it! Once the truth is uncovered, the realization that we NEED God's DEEP healing and NOT just 'topical tending' is paramount. For me, bringing these facts to light seemed to 'just happen' during EMDR and with other therapies. With the TRUTH of the past brought to the surface and exposed, much backlash followed.

One horrific memory after another, on the heels of 'escaping' my 'surrogate abuser[10] husband'; suddenly, the gal with all the emotions, was all over the place with FEELINGS. Our entire, and I do mean ENTIRE family felt the IMPACT. There are times, I found, when 'breaking strongholds' in families, fear is felt, which manifests itself as anger. NOT BEING BELIEVED by my mother was heartbreaking, as well as alienating. Reoccurring somatically felt memories of *her* dad's violent assaults during this period; *keeping my head above water was the best I could do* for 18 long months.

---

[9] The Bible Project: Tim Mackie and Jon Collins (long-time friends and one-time roommates at Multnomah University) work together to help people read through Scripture while avoiding the common pitfalls and misunderstandings. They present complex biblical themes in a way that is real and unapologetic but approachable. With Tim's deep biblical understanding and Jon's passion for visual storytelling, they started creating videos in 2014 and put them online for free. BibleProject is a registered 501©3nonprofit organization and has been fully crowdfunded from the beginning. https://bibleproject.com > tim-mackie

[10] SURROGATE ABUSER: The person, in our victimization, we find as a new villain (real or imagined) to complete our victim cycle. Done inadvertently in our trauma wounds.

Feelings of what is perceived as betrayal are frequently expressed by family members when such ugly truths are brought to light. These truths had been hidden and kept hushed; they had laid dormant for years until someone cracked. And that someone was me…literally.

I have seen how bitterness can corrode relationships. Satan wants us to fight each other on all fronts, keeping us in a state of confusion. Add a few layers of trauma by both parties, Satan can sit back and watch the friction bubble and boil. Coming to terms with our past is dreadfully difficult, fighting the demons that have haunted us for years; the healing feels tenuous at best, and a harsh word can bring months of therapy crashing around your ankles. We mustn't let the enemy gain ground back. We want freedom for those family members who are still hiding behind 'family pride' or 'generational secrets' or 'internal lies' FOR SELF-PRESERVATION. The more FREEDOM I felt in my body, soul, and Spirit, the more I wanted the same for my mom. In the end, sadly, we cannot control another's healing. *But we can choose OUR response.*

Fighting the lies that were thrown at me THROUGH WOUNDS never addressed or healed, my mom could bring me to my knees. To say this was disheartening and difficult would be an understatement. But, unexpectedly, with GOD'S GRACE, I no longer saw an angry mom, I saw MY MOM. A woman afraid and lost in the agony of this fallen world we live in, like me, just trying to muddle through and unsure of the next step. I felt the unhealed wounds that my mom still carries. My mom lived my life…but I suspected, it no doubt, was so much more than I could know. Her pain ran as deep as mine had run. My eyes of GRACE could see my mom in a whole new way. Praise YOU, GOD, for eyes to see, a SPIRIT to understand, and a HEART to feel the pain shared.

(Ephesians 4:29-32 ESV) Let no corrupting talk come out of your mouths, but only such as is good for building up, as fits the occasion, that it may give grace to those who hear. And do not grieve the Holy Spirit of God, by whom you were sealed for the day of redemption. Let all bitterness and wrath and anger and clamor and slander be put away from you, along with all malice. Be kind to one another, tenderhearted, forgiving one another, as GOD IN CHRIST FORGAVE YOU.

I truly believe this is where GOD ushers in the next generation of more enlightened women, knowing God's truth always shines light into the darkness of secrets kept; healing and giving grace to those that continue to struggle. (Eph. 5:8-11 ESV); for at one time you were darkness, but now you are light in the Lord. Walk as children of light (for the fruit of light is found in all that is good and right and true) and try to discern what is pleasing to the Lord. Take no part in the unfruitful works of darkness, but instead expose them. 'Therefore, be IMITATORS OF GOD, as beloved children. And walk in love, as Christ loved us and gave himself up for us, a fragrant offering and sacrifice to God.' (Ephesians 5:1-2 ESV)

We Serve A Generational God

For at one time you were darkness, but now you are light in the Lord. Walk as children of light.

Ephesians 5:8

Can God count on me to be this 'next generation' to usher in the light that shines in the darkness of secrets kept? _____

_____

_____

THE STORM HAS A PURPOSE

"Take heart; it is I. Do not be afraid." Matthew 14:27

Stepping out in FAITH as we MUST do to conquer our fears and face what has held us in chains is frightening. (And Peter answered Him, "Lord if it is You, command me to come to you on the water." He said, "Come." So, Peter got out of the boat and walked on the water and came to Jesus. Matthew 14:28,29 ESV)

LIKE PETER, WE NEED THAT 'COMMAND' FROM JESUS TO MOVE US FORWARD ON OUR WALK into the murky waters of our PAST. And once underway, the commitment is made. This healing and wholeness God wants for us seems merciless and is not without peril. *This perseverance in FAITH is no small ask.* From the longevity of the processing, the nightmares, the setbacks, and the naysayers; we find ourselves descending into the darkness frequently. (But when he saw the wind, he was afraid, and beginning to sink he cried out, "Lord, save me." Jesus immediately reached out His hand and took hold of him saying to him, "O you of little faith, why did you doubt?" and when they got into the boat, the wind ceased. And those in the boat worshipped Him, saying, "Truly You are the Son of God." Matthew 14:30-33 ESV)

It is when our eyes are focused on all that is around us ('when he [Peter] saw the wind') that we succumb to fear and anxiety. When the waves of life seem too mighty; the negative thoughts want to overtake us and the demons want to dance in the halls at lights out: CRY TO JESUS.

KEEP JESUS CLOSE. Reach out to HIM. Focus on Jesus, forcing ourselves to set our sights on the only thing that matters…HIS HAND REACHING OUT TO OURS. He wants nothing more than to hold us in our fear. His closeness blocks out all the background chaos, noise, and confusion as He pulls us closer still. As our souls unite, this is the PEACE that is felt through communion with JESUS, THE SON OF GOD.

I will step-out in faith into the murky waters of my past. Jesus, help me with all the chaos that is bombarding me. Today I am struggling with... _____

_____
_____
_____
_____
_____

KEEP JESUS CLOSE. REACH OUT TO HIM.

Rejoice

Nothing in all of creation will separate me from love of God in Christ Jesus our Lord.
Romans 8:39

I will NOT leave you or forsake you.
Joshua 1:5

"Take heart; it is I. Do not be afraid."
Matthew 14:27

God is good.

Rejoice in the Lord. Trust in HIM.

...God, remind me You are bigger than my fears...

Write a short prayer for freedom of what I am struggling with today. _____

_____
_____
_____ — Amen.

OUR TRIBE MATTERS

Your vibe attracts your tribe.

I FIND IT FASCINATING TO CONSIDER THE CHOICE OF THE APOSTLES. JESUS HAND-PICKED who would follow Him, and help Him in His ministry, even knowing He traveled with a traitor in His midst. Yet, Judas is THAT MAN who would set God's plan into action.

The ones we surround ourselves with MATTER. When life goes sideways, NO DOUBT, a time when we are thankful our support system is in place. That is certainly how I felt during the years of 'TRAUMA RECOVERY'.

Proverbs 17:7 (ESV) A friend loves at all times, and a brother/SISTER IS BORN OUT OF ADVERSITY. My support, the friends in my Bible Study, my close friend Jodi, those who held me through my storm: These SISTERS: MY TRIBE, that walked the tiresome and oh-so-frightening journey have chiseled a place in my heart. I believe there is much truth to the fact that it is not so much the trauma you EXPERIENCED, but the fact that you felt VERY MUCH ALONE during and ESPECIALLY after the experience. ("Children don't get traumatized because they get hurt, they get traumatized because *they're ALONE with the hurt.*" Dr. Gabor Matè)[11] Granted rape at the hands of grandpa and boy/men IS an experience that sets one up for a lifetime of feeling DIFFERENT and ALONE. As a little, handling such a 'BIG' adult, and very life-threatening, 'grown-up' feeling, with NO ADULT SUPERVISION led to a less-than-healthy outcome. Having validation from those in this group, I felt anything but ALONE. This is not to say there is not an exodus of some. As

---

[11] Dr. Gabor Maté: Physician and Author with a background in Family Medicine and a special interest in childhood development and TRAUMA; with its potential lifelong impacts on physical and mental health in correlation to autoimmune disease, cancer, ADHD, addictions, and a wide range of other conditions. Author of five books including SCATTERED MINDS: New Look at the Origins and Healing of Attention Deficit Disorder, WHEN THE BODY SAYS NO: The Cost of Hidden Stress, and his newest book; THE MYTH OF NORMAL: Trauma, Illness, and Healing in a Toxic Culture.

discoveries flood, relationships are strained. Truly, healing is an ALL-ENCOMPASSING undertaking. Like many trauma survivors, I learned that not all we are close to are adept at handling the intensity and longevity of the processing of one's life during this horrific experience. (And…this is not to say, that wounded people have not attracted our fair share of wounded friends.) In some way or another, we all live out of our past. As I have moved through the remainder of my healing, feeling anything but alone, with my husband and my faithful friends, I am reminded of a story told. Our support in our lives is like that of a tree…I tend to picture a giant oak; mighty, having weathered many harsh storms. The leaves on that fine tree are many, and prolific, teaming with insects, squirrels, and birds. The color change is beautiful in autumn, and the vividness is suddenly replaced by barrenness. The realization that these leaves are just 'FILLERS', and will be replaced every spring with 'NEW FILLERS'. But those branches; look at the STRENGTH in those mighty branches, especially those larger ones. Having been there for years, they have strength and stature. YES, they have stood the 'test' of time. Those will be there forever, no doubt, those are branches I could build on, I'm certain. If I climb onto one of those stronger branches, I think I will step out further, a little further still… 'SNAP', *I stepped too far*; I went too far, and that branch just couldn't hold all that I had to carry. The ROOTS, *those deep-reaching roots*. That is where, my friend, our strength comes from, those are where God gives us the strength to flourish, to continue, even in the driest season; those large roots down there, those are the ones that are feeding us when nothing else can, when we are in that drought. When we're in that dry spell when nothing else seems to keep us alive, the friends ONLY GOD could have placed in our lives. Those are our 'ROOT FRIENDS', our 'PRAYER WARRIORS', 'OUR SUPPORT SYSTEM': OUR GOD PEOPLE!

A friend loves at all times, and a sister is born out of adversity. Proverbs 17:7

Who have been my 'Root Friends', my God people through my hard, dry season?

_____
_____
_____
_____
_____

Every Story Is Sacred

If you see beauty in someone – speak it and above all, be all in

Know this, my beloved brothers: let every person be quick to hear, slow to speak, slow to anger… James 1:19 ESV.

EVERYONE'S STORY IS SACRED. LET THEM TELL IT. BE SLOW TO RESPOND. LISTEN AND LEARN. As our stories are being told, many also want to share theirs. Everyone's life is important and relevant, everyone has A SACRED STORY TO TELL. BE THE PERSON that is present for them. Save that child from *battling for attention* for the rest of their life; listen with COMPASSION to their burdens and struggles, *NOW*, and show them the respect and the worthiness they deserve. DO NOT dishonor them when they choose to share with you by being disrespectful or worse DISMISSIVE. We are to REFLECT God's CHARACTER and bring HIM GLORY in our GRACIOUS words. Through my life's happenings, in a WORLD OF IMPERFECTION, I have realized how much we are all connected in our suffering, loss, deep pain, and joy. As we share our triumphs as well as those defeats: Connection and authenticity ARE GOD'S PLAN FOR THIS WORLD. True relationships are joining one another through the SACREDNESS of the journey God calls us to walk. Not just our past moments of 'glory' but our 'now' moments that He IS CALLING US TO ACTION. Be available for that call to action. Pick up the nuances of a cry to be heard, whether it be a misbehaving child, a wayward teen, or the silence of a friend. Truly we all just need to be heard and acknowledged. *Before passing judgment on someone who seems to be self-destructing, consider what might be inside them that they are trying to destroy.* My powerful healing through the presence and GRACE OF MY PEOPLE during times of turmoil and self-sabotage led me to discover the unfailing STRENGTH, incomparable WISDOM, and the infinite LOVE OF A PERFECT GOD. We all have a story to tell.

I'll go one step further…More importantly, God wants us all to be heard as we cry for HELP IN OUR HEALING!

Do nothing from selfish ambition or conceit, but in humility count others more significant than yourselves. Let each of you look not only to his own interests but also to the interests of others. Philippians 2:3,4 (ESV)

EVERY STORY IS SACRED

If you see beauty in someone—Speak it—And above all—Be all in!

...BE QUICK TO HEAR, SLOW TO SPEAK, SLOW TO ANGER...
JAMES 1:19

Our gracious words reflect God's character.

Do nothing from selfish ambition or conceit, but in humility count others more significant than yourselves.
Let each of you look not only to his own interests but also to the interests of others.
Philippians 2:3,4

SELF-LOVE THROUGH GOD'S LOVE

"Stand your ground, it's sacred." Janelle Suggs

A CHILD IS NOT BUILT TO BEAR THE WEIGHT OF ALL THAT IS PLACED UPON THEM FROM trauma experienced. The negative impact on the brain 'wiring' with all its ugly psychological baggage causes an abundance of issues. Children who were deprived in one way or another of the safety needed, either physical or emotional, do not respond by turning away or disliking their caregivers. Sadly, our internal need for approval and people-pleasing runs deep because unfortunately, we turn our hurt and dislike INWARD ON OURSELVES. Self-love can feel extremely complicated, almost impossible throughout adulthood until we understand where this originates from—being *invalidated or dismissed as children* (or *even as adults* as we sort out the wreckage of our past) brings its own level of demoralization, self-loathing, and trauma. For me, it was through therapy, I realized I didn't want to be 'invisible' any longer. I didn't want to blend into societal norms, pretending to be 'OKAY' or to be 'FINE'. I wanted to be SEEN and HEARD, VISIBLE to the important people in my life. As all my ugly 'YUCK' came to light, 'what was dark was brought into the LIGHT', I wanted to share, not so my people close to me would hurt too, but in hopes of expelling the stigma, the shame that I had lived in for most of my life. As healing seems lengthy, painful, and isolating, discouragement sets in. We must bear in mind, YES, that trauma changes our brains in negative ways, but HEALING brings POSITIVE changes to our brains. We can change! Perhaps for the first time, *I felt I deserved validation to breathe the same air as the 'NORMAL' people.* Only to find out some still wanted to "Stomp down" what I had to say because of its ugliness.

This is where we must recognize the huge price to be paid as a 'Cycle Breaker'. A choice must be made as we choose to disrupt dysfunctional family behavior *IN OURSELVES*. This starts the process of healing in the family, however, in the wake of change, some choose to sit on the shore and find fault, while others paddle in the opposite direction. If I silently remained 'changed' without becoming too vocal, without becoming too empowered, or too independent all was as it should be. But try as I might, this was not who God created me to be. I seem to find myself living out Luke 12:2-3…

"Nothing is covered up that will not be revealed or hidden that will not be known. Therefore, whatever you have said in the dark shall be heard in the light, and what you have whispered in private rooms shall be proclaimed on the housetops." Luke 12:2-3 (ESV)

For me, I fought 'tooth and nail' assuming I was breaking some horrifying familial 'curse' that had held my family in chains for years. Until the day I slowed long enough for God to help me realize…I had raised my 8 children doing EXACTLY THE OPPOSITE to the way I was raised. Where anger and bullying were commonplace; *we prayed for bullies*. Broken objects were cause for anger flare-ups and cursing in my childhood home. These were just 'things', and *children's feelings were always given more care* under my roof. And most importantly, *children were protected at all costs*. I may not have remembered the assaults of my youth until much later; but I certainly knew children, MY children were my most guarded gift. I would, at all costs, protect them.

Suddenly, *I realized I HAD BROKEN THE CYCLE OF VIOLENCE*. My children were raised in a home quite the opposite of the domineering, oppressive, temper-filled house that I grew up in. We lived a life of peace, for the most part, and most certainly lived a GRACE-FILLED life.

Nothing is covered up that will not be revealed, or hidden that will not be known. Therefore whatever you have said in the dark shall be heard in the light, and what you have whispered in private rooms shall be proclaimed on the housetops.

Luke 12:2,3

How have I chosen to deal with my trauma? Internally? Or a more vocal approach? How has it been received? This makes me feel?

_____

_____

_____

_____

_____

_____

WE WERE BORN TO BE REAL, NOT PERFECT

Make today so awesome – yesterday gets jealous.

For by grace, you have been saved through faith. And this is not your own doing; it is a gift of God, not a result of works, so that no one may boast. For we are His workmanship, created in Christ Jesus for good works, which God prepared beforehand, that we should walk in them. Ephesians 2:8 (ESV)

I BELIEVE THE SOONER WE LEARN TO LIVE OUR LIVES OUT OF A BELIEF THAT 'I AM perfectly imperfect, saved through the blood of Jesus Christ, My Savior', the sooner we can live our lives authentically. For me, and dare I say most, we have existed to please, first our parents, then our teachers and coaches, our bosses, and the list goes on. Even to the point, of living a life, working to gain God's favor. As if, a scoreboard in the sky keeps a tally of our achievements to be presented at our death, waiting for the 'nod from the BIG GUY'. All the while, God patiently woos us to Himself, accepting us as HE CREATED US TO BE. We needn't toil to win His favor. As I have painstakingly, peeled back layer after layer of what the 'world' has placed on me, and finding the 'real me' that GOD created deep inside has been an epic journey. I have discovered 'OUR JULIE' in the process: God's Julie needn't put on a mask. I am loveable. I am worthy of that love. My blessings are many. God gifted me with those many gifts…We worked TOGETHER to uncover the 'original' that is ME. My passage away from disguising my fears in attempts at perfection in search of authenticity has led to new insights. There were many days I felt faulty and broken beyond repair. One such day, being sweetly reminded by my husband, *"That's how the light gets in!"* (Leonard Cohen) My journey has led me back to ME. GRATITUDE IS IN ORDER! And all glory and honor to MY CREATOR.

Have I reached a point in my healing and my life where I need to re-examine how I am living my life? Who am I 'trying to please' and why? Have I peeled my mask off and gotten vulnerable with myself? What are my many gifts? Listing them helps! How have these gifts Helped in my fight through trauma to freedom? I need to be gentle and generous with myself…I am made in the likeness of God, for good works.

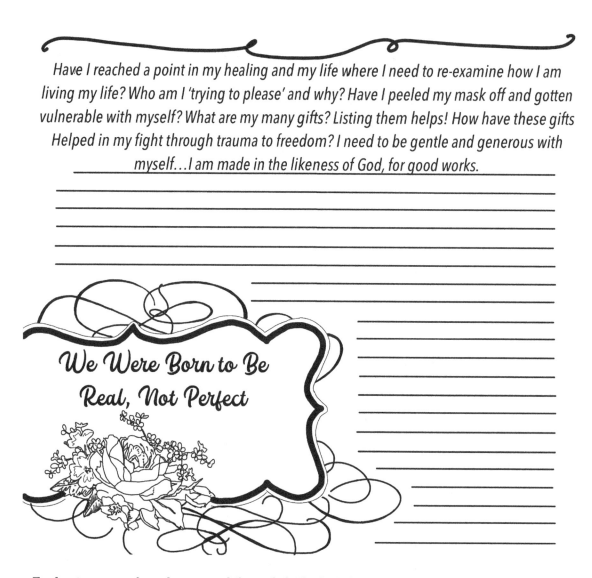

We Were Born to Be
Real, Not Perfect

For by grace, you have been saved through faith. And this is not your own doing; it is a gift of God, not a result of works, so that no one may boast. For we are His workmanship, created in Christ Jesus for good works, which God prepared beforehand, that we should walk in them.
Ephesians 2:8

OUR CALL TO THE LIGHT

Don't let your fear dictate your day or decide your fate.

1 PETER 2:9 (ESV) BUT YOU ARE A CHOSEN RACE, A ROYAL PRIESTHOOD A HOLY NATION, a people for His own possession, that you may proclaim the excellencies of Him who called you out of darkness into His marvelous light.

I love this scripture. Yes, everything about it! I believe for those who have lived under the cloak of unworthiness, in the darkness that has been nipping at our heels threatening to devour us and pull us under to a sinking abyss, never feeling quite like we were good enough, or never actually fitting into this world of 'normal'; these words wiped the slate clean. Here we are told, that not only are we CHOSEN, ROYAL, and HOLY; we are HIS POSSESSION as well. How wonderful to have this glorious sense of belonging. With these words, I WANT TO PROCLAIM HIS EXCELLENCIES! To finally be led out of the dreadful darkness of depression, unworthiness, and shame and called into HIS marvelous LIGHT. That being said, the process of belonging to HIS CHOSEN HOLY NATION comes with much sacrifice and hardship. I wondered as I looked back on my life of 'MUCH'; was I made 'strong in my weakness'? Was my 'FAITH powerful enough'? Was my 'trust sufficient' to produce obedience? I saw how my faith wavered in the present as I maneuvered toward the future; knowing all the while the end goal IS OBEDIENCE TO GOD THE FATHER. And yet, HOPE...ALWAYS HOPE IN JESUS... Therefore, since we are surrounded, by so great a cloud of witnesses, let us lay aside every weight and sin which clings so closely, and let us run with endurance the race that is set before us, looking to Jesus, the founder, and perfecter of our faith, who for the joy that was set before Him, He endured the cross, despising the shame, and is seated at the right hand of the throne of God. Hebrews 12: 1,2 (ESV) As we 'work out' our pasts, our lives, and our relationship with God, Jesus sits to the right of God, keenly aware, empathizing I'd guess, our angst to get it 'right', forgetting, as we tend to do, GOD LOVES US JUST 'CAUSE HE LOVES US! And once again, peace seeps in, the brow unfurrows, and our Spirit rests in His love.

In Him was life, and the life was the light of men. The light shines in the darkness, and the darkness has NOT overcome it. John 1:5 (ESV)

Our Call To Light

In Him was life, and the life was the light of men. The light shines in the darkness, and the darkness has not overcome it.
John 1:5

As healing continues, am I feeling a lightening in my Spirit? _____

_____

But you are a chosen race, a royal priesthood, a holy nation, a people for His own possession, that you may proclaim the excellencies of Him who called you out of darkness into His marvelous light.   1 Peter 2:9

LET YOUR HURT LEAD YOU TO THE HEALER

First, feed your soul.

Now I see the driest season of my life was when my spiritual strength developed the most. When my emotional pain was the deepest, the Lord seemed to hold His hand out to me. O LORD, my strength and my stronghold, my refuge in the day of trouble, to you shall the nations come... Jeremiah 16:19 (ESV)

"Blessed is the man who trusts in the LORD, whose trust is the LORD." Jeremiah 17:7 (ESV) Many days were spent with my Bible, asking God for answers. The biggest question possibly was, "Where are you God, in all this ugliness?" At this point in my process, my best friend and I were no longer speaking. Whether we triggered each other in our wounds, or possibly, we were meant only to be friends for a season, or my childhood trauma-fest was lasting entirely too long, I will never know; nonetheless, I felt alone and STUCK. We can choose to fight, kick, and scream, or open those tightly clenched fists and gently let our friends go, knowing childhood sexual assault is dreadful. No one should be FORCED to process such violence except those who MUST. *Those of us who did not choose our dreadful path, yet bravely confronted and faced what life had thrown our way; taking God's hand as HE led us through our healing process, as we trusted HIM for strength, patience, and perseverance. Ultimately, realizing life is not always good, BUT GOD IS ALWAYS GOOD.*

My relationship with God was not a fickle love, He remained steady and true; continually guiding me to scripture that soothed my soul. Self-discovery is painful, but living with unconscious wounds holds its pain, and a fair portion of fear. The person I became *cost me* relationships, old patterns, and old behaviors; but the gain is generational healing. Romans

8:28 (ESV) And we know that for those who love God, all things work together for good for those who are called according to His purpose.

Our purpose can be heavy, but sacred work is rarely light I would assume. Thank you, LORD, for trusting me with this sacred work.

Sometimes, we do not choose our dreadful path, yet bravely confronted and faced what life had thrown our way. Taking God's hand as He led us through our healing process, we trusted Him for strength, patience, and perseverance. Ultimately, realizing life is not always good, but GOD IS ALWAYS GOOD.

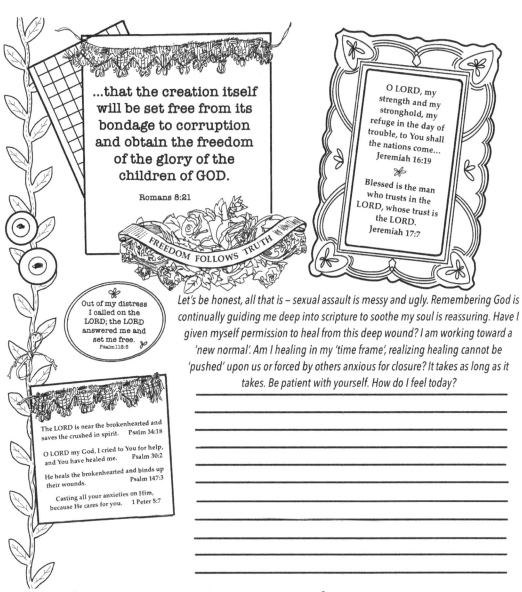

...that the creation itself will be set free from its bondage to corruption and obtain the freedom of the glory of the children of GOD.

Romans 8:21

FREEDOM FOLLOWS TRUTH

O LORD, my strength and my stronghold, my refuge in the day of trouble, to You shall the nations come...
Jeremiah 16:19

Blessed is the man who trusts in the LORD, whose trust is the LORD.
Jeremiah 17:7

Out of my distress I called on the LORD; the LORD answered me and set me free.
Psalm 118:5

The LORD is near the brokenhearted and saves the crushed in spirit.   Psalm 34:18

O LORD my God, I cried to You for help, and You have healed me.   Psalm 30:2

He heals the brokenhearted and binds up their wounds.   Psalm 147:3

Casting all your anxieties on Him, because He cares for you.   1 Peter 5:7

Let's be honest, all that is – sexual assault is messy and ugly. Remembering God is continually guiding me deep into scripture to soothe my soul is reassuring. Have I given myself permission to heal from this deep wound? I am working toward a 'new normal'. Am I healing in my 'time frame', realizing healing cannot be 'pushed' upon us or forced by others anxious for closure? It takes as long as it takes. Be patient with yourself. How do I feel today?

_____
_____
_____
_____
_____
_____
_____
_____
_____
_____
_____

Lord, I ask for Your help in healing the secret places. The deep wounds that some do not understand take much care and time to mend. Feeling, as well as believing, I am safe and whole is a tall order. Step into my heart as I pray today for peace and freedom. In Your name, Jesus, I ask this with all humility. Amen.

ACKNOWLEDGE ANGER

Freedom always follows truth.

ALONG MY LONG, ROCKY ROAD TO HEALING, I REALIZED THAT I STRUGGLED TO LAY HOLD of my anger for quite some time. With much of my life keeping everyone 'happy and contented' at all costs, anger was an energy wasted, one I rarely had time to allow in my life of 'HAPPY'. I began to realize *my anger had turned inward to shame, a defense mechanism and a developmental aftereffect of trauma*; one that I had truly never released for fear of leaving myself entirely too vulnerable. Vulnerability was a position I had been in before and feared above all else. Yet avoidance only prolongs the suffering, and until we own our emotions, they consequently OWN US. We need to realize that we are not at fault for what we endured, BUT we are the only ones who can release ourselves from the hold the shame has on our lives. By giving ourselves the respect and kindness that we DESERVED THEN, and *PERMISSION* to grieve the reality of what happened to us in the past, we can consequently move forward in our healing. For me, this grieving period seemed to last an eternity, and I needed much reminding that healing from childhood sexual abuse takes much time and is not linear in its course. Rushing and pushing for closure from well-meaning friends and family led to *oppressive feelings of once again living in a powerless state of submission.* Forgiveness COMES, I BELIEVE, but for me, the grieving needed to come first. There were days my Therapist sent me a 'homework list'; discovering later, that it was in the unprescribed sloppy, messy cry in my husband's arms later that week that I would release the bulk of my oppressive feelings of sadness and pain. Knowing my husband could dry the recurrent and very persistent tears helped expel much grief, but for true HEALING I WOULD PULL FROM SCRIPTURE AS ULTIMATELY MY HOPE COMES FROM THE LORD.

Psalm 147:3 (ESV) He heals the brokenhearted and binds up their wounds. 1 Peter 5:7 (ESV) Casting all your anxieties on Him, because He cares for you. 1 Peter 5:10 (ESV) And after you have suffered a little while, the God of all grace, who has called you to his eternal glory in Christ, will Himself restore, confirm, strengthen, and establish you.

Psalm 34:18 (ESV) The LORD is near the brokenhearted and saves the crushed in spirit. Psalm 30:2 (ESV) O LORD my God, I cried to You for help, and You have healed me.

Acknowledge Anger

Whether my anger is hard to contain or has turned inward to shame, it must be dealt with. Avoidance prolongs the suffering. Am I showing myself the kindness I deserved back then? Have I given myself permission to grieve the reality of what happened? Am I reminding myself, "It takes as long as it takes"? Pushing for closure can bring oppressive feelings; be gentle in the process.

_____
_____
_____
_____
_____
_____
_____
_____

The LORD is near the brokenhearted and saves the crushed in spirit. Psalm 34:18

O LORD, my God, I cried to You for help, and You have healed me.   Psalm 30:2

ANCHORED IN GRACE

While His grace flooded my heart

"*It's okay to be scared...you're about to do something BRAVE*". I remember reading this at some point in my process of recovery, thinking, "That's for SURE!" This journey of UNBECOMING all that has been layered on abuse survivors IS SCARY. It takes stamina, courage, the continual support of our faithful friends, therapy (I believe), and FAITH grounded in GOD'S GRACE. Many days, if not for God's grace, there was NO BRAVERY, NO FIGHT inside of me. It was truly in promises made throughout scripture that held me.

"The Lord be with your spirit. Grace be with you." 2 Timothy 4:22 (ESV) "Likewise the Spirit helps us in our weakness. For we do not know what to pray for as we ought, but the SPIRIT HIMSELF intercedes for us with groanings too deep for words." Romans 8:26 (ESV)

"Be strong and courageous. Do not be afraid or terrified because of them, for the Lord your God goes with you; He will never leave you or forsake you." Deuteronomy 31:6 (ESV)

"Be strong and courageous, because you will lead these people to inherit the land I swore to their ancestors to give them." Joshua 1:6 (ESV) "Have I not commanded you? Be strong and courageous. Do not be afraid; do not be discouraged, for your God will be with you wherever you go." Joshua 1:9 (ESV)

"Be on guard; stand firm in the faith; be courageous; be strong." 1 Corinthians 16:13 (ESV) "Be strong and take heart, all you who hope in the Lord." Psalm 31:24 (ESV)

"So do not fear, for I am with you; do not be dismayed, for I am your God. I will strengthen you and help you; I will uphold you with my righteous right hand." Isaiah 41:10 (ESV)

"For God gave us a spirit not of fear, but of power, love, and self-control." 2 Timothy 1:7 (ESV) "But you, take courage! Do not let your hands be weak, for your work shall be rewarded." 2 Chronicles 15:7 (ESV) "Wait for the Lord; be strong, and let your heart take courage; wait for the Lord!" Psalm 27:14 (ESV)

It is in KNOWING that GOD'S GRACE is the anchor that holds us firmly in place when we feel adrift in our feelings, our pain, and our over-the-top fear. He is our continual stronghold through it all.

"So do not fear, for I am with you; do not be dismayed, for I am your God. I will strengthen you and help you; I will uphold you with my righteous right hand."

Isaiah 41:10

"For God gave us a spirit not of fear, but of power, love, and self control."

2 Timothy 1:7

"Likewise the Spirit helps us in our weakness. For we do not know what to pray for as we ought, but the SPIRIT HIMSELF intercedes for us with groaning too deep for words."

Romans 8:26

I know that God's Grace is the anchor that holds me firmly in place when I feel adrift in my feelings, pain, and over-the-top fear. Remembering YOU are my continual stronghold, I still struggle, Lord, even as I hold firmly to your promise. Let me vent all that seems to swirl around me. Take all of this to Your Throneroom…

In Jesus name I pray… _____

_____

_____

_____

_____

_____

_____

_____

_____

_____

_____

_____

LIVE LIFE PURPOSEFULLY

Your life unfolds in proportion to your courage.

SEEK GOD IN ALL YOU DO. MAKE LIFE LESS ABOUT PERFORMANCE AND MORE ABOUT listening to that small still voice inside that whispers and pushes us out of our comfort zone and into God's calling. Some have lived their lives ducking feelings or keeping them inside, not wanting to 'compete' with all the 'BIG FEELINGS' around them. For some, even in the houses we grew up in, there was simply no room for our feelings. We remained silent. Now, moving into this 'NEW CREATION' OR is it rediscovering MYSELF and finding my voice, I realize it can lead me astray much of the time. Mine wanted to circle back to disorder and turmoil after so many years of holding tight to dreadful 'feelings'. The key here is seeking God's voice of calmness always, in all circumstances. For God is not a God of confusion but of peace. 1 Corinthians 14:33 (ESV)

If there is one thing I have learned, not only from my therapist and books read but from my personal experience; loss of childhood innocence affects us deeply. As I have experienced the fall-out, all the residual effects suffered to my personality as well as physically felt, I know this as factual. But what I also KNOW is when my mind defaults to shame, as it still can do occasionally, when it wants to tell me I am flawed, unacceptable, and unworthy I can immediately shift my mind in a new direction, amend my thoughts, divert them to God's GOODNESS and GRACE. Where there is GRACE, there is GOD: THIS I KNOW. Always being PURPOSEFUL; turning my whole body, if need be, as well as my thoughts in a new direction.

FEELINGS: God gave them to me in triplicate, but I must learn how to contend with them at that moment...OR after the fact...WITH THE AFTEREFFECTS. I decided to take the more direct route; turn to GOD, turn AWAY from *'MY BULLY: MY BRAIN'*. Fight strategically, this internal battle of my brain. I was truly realizing...I held no grudge or hatred for any of my abusers, for anyone that misplaced me and 'let' these attacks happen or 'left' me to be raped. This remaining 'KIND IN A CRUEL SITUATION' and living filled with GRACE, my life's longing: to live like JESUS... PURPOSEFUL, was hindered by not giving MYSELF GRACE. It seemed to me giving others grace was far easier than dolling it out for myself. Fortunately, GOD'S LOVE BREAKS ALL BARRIERS...even those that we erected years ago when the lies spoken over me seeped in a took me over. I know my God does NOT want me to live out of confusion and chaos but in His purpose for me, in GRACE. I must say here, and my therapist will agree, THIS IS DIFFICULT: To unlearn, old thoughts, and old habits, and to genuinely find peace with our violent pasts. But praise GOD IT IS POSSIBLE with much hard work and the Spirit working through us.

For my thoughts are not your thoughts, neither are your ways my ways, declares the LORD. For as the heavens are higher than the earth, so are my ways higher than your ways and my thoughts than your thoughts. Isaiah 55:8,9 (ESV)

Isaiah 55:8,9

For my thoughts are not your thoughts, neither are your ways my ways, declares the LORD. For as the heavens are higher than the earth, so are my ways higher than your ways and my thoughts than your thoughts.

Remember that remaining kind in a cruel situation and living GRACE FILLED means living PURPOSEFUL.

REMAKE OUR MINDS

Declare it.

OUR NEGATIVE THOUGHTS AND DOUBTS SIMPLY CAN NOT STAND UP TO THE LIGHT OF God's TRUTH. Focusing on what is noble, pure, and right (Philippians 4:8 ESV) is a must. Our thoughts MATTER if we are to heal from our painful pasts and move into a FUTURE OF HOPE, FORGIVENESS, AND TRUE TRANSFORMATION.

"Do not be conformed to this world, but be transformed by the renewal of your mind, that by testing you may discern what is the will of God, what is good and acceptable and perfect." Romans 12:2 (ESV)

But more importantly, we are told to 'Put off our old self, which belongs to your former manner of life and is corrupt through deceitful desires, and to be renewed in the spirit of your minds, and to put on the new self, created after the likeness of God in true righteousness and holiness.' (Ephesians 4:22-24 ESV)

These scriptures seemed to bring such hope for me as I struggled with the yuck that wanted to occupy my mind; I could counter-attack with all that was PURE AND LOVELY. When doubt assailed my senses, I would remind myself through the words in scripture, NO, I am 'created after the likeness of God in true righteousness and holiness.' Meditating on the PRAISEWORTHY brings us back into alignment with God's purpose for us and ultimately HIS DEEP LOVE AND PEACE SETTLES OUR SOUL.

"Finally, brothers (and sisters), whatever is true, whatever is honorable, whatever is pure, whatever is lovely, whatever is commendable, if there is any excellence, if there is anything worthy of praise, think about these things." Philippians 4:8 (ESV) …And suddenly…all that seemed tangled, is straightened, all that was sinking, feels weightless...my thoughts take me to PEACE.

"See how very much our Father loves us, for He calls us His children, and that is what we are!" 1 John 3:1a (ESV) AMEN.

REMAKE
our
MINDS

"Do not be conformed to this world, but be transformed by the renewal of your mind, that by testing you may discern what is the will of God, what is good and acceptable and perfect."

Romans 12:2

"Put off our old self, which belongs to your former manner of life and is corrupt through deceitful desires, and to be renewed in the spirit of your minds, and to put on the new self, created after the likeness of God in true righteousness and holiness.

Ephesians 4:22- 24

DECLARE IT!

EMBRACING EMOTIONS

Not over, not under, but through them

TO A LARGE DEGREE, OUR HAPPINESS AND THE QUALITY OF OUR LIVES REST ON THE quality of our THOUGHTS. And our thoughts are very often influenced by our EMOTIONS. Understanding, all the while, that God gave us emotions to alert us that something NEEDS TO BE ADDRESSED. Here is where we bring God into our feelings. I've learned to stop trying to numb or vent or stomp out the anger and fear and every other emotion that wants to fly at me; rather *MANAGE MY REACTION* to these emotions. Here I will admit, my emotions want to steam-roll me. My emotions left to their own devices grow bigger than life. For one who in the past tried keeping these larger-than-life feelings boxed for the protection of all, I NOW realize *they need to be dealt with*. Therapy has taught me much. The goal, I have learned from Matt, is what he calls a *"window of tolerance"* which is sandwiched between hyperarousal and hypo arousal: this window, *my target, as I continue through healing (and life).* When we are in the 'window of tolerance' it is smooth sailing; we are handling what is being thrown our way, be it life in general, or triggering memories. It is when we react in an uncharacteristic way or in contrast to what a situation might call for; becoming very angry or conversely sinking into a depressive state that we need to regulate ourselves once again. Ultimately, GOD WANTS us to live peaceably with Him as well as all others, BUT *to do this we must first find OUR PEACE.*

It is in realizing that feelings are just that, FEELINGS. Embrace them, unravel and decipher them, and interpret what God is helping reveal to us. Remember, God is for us, He is not against us. He wants us whole and healthy to carry out the plans HE HAS FOR US. He knows the REAL YOU underneath the layers. Listen to what He is saying to you. Jeremiah 29:11 (ESV) For I know the plans I have for you, declares the LORD, plans for welfare and not for evil, to give you a future and a hope.

It is in feeling the emotions, contending with them that God is helping us discern the next action that needs to be taken, or for that matter, NOT TO BE TAKEN. Philippians 4:6-7 (ESV) reminds us to bring those emotions TO GOD IN PRAYER. ...do not be anxious about anything, but in everything by prayer and supplication with thanksgiving let your requests be made known to God. And the peace of God which surpasses all understanding will guard your hearts and your minds in Christ Jesus. Isn't it wonderful to worship a God who helps us sort through even those hard feelings others find pesky, confusing, or downright unrelatable?

EMBRACE EMOTIONS
NOT OVER, NOT UNDER, BUT THROUGH THEM

Understanding that my emotions must be addressed and managed; what is bothering me currently? Am I keeping my emotions in the 'window of tolerance'? _____

_____

_____

_____

_____

_____

SETBACKS AND STUMBLING BLOCKS

Comeback kid

WHO DOESN'T LOVE A COMEBACK STORY? WHERE, AGAINST ALL ODDS, SOMEONE BATTLES against, seemingly impossible odds to fight for victory. The Bible is full of stories of these victorious accounts. Joseph, Jacob, Moses, Peter, goodness…even Samson was victorious in the impossible position *he put himself in.* Of course, the greatest 'COMEBACK STORY' ever, Jesus' coming back from the dead and rising to new life! *Talk about HOPE for the hopeless.*

Some days the question posed to God, in all sincerity, "I AM THANKFUL, I've made it this far, BUT HOW MUCH LONGER? How can I come back from all that is sinking me presently?" I know God is for me. "But, God, another trigger to alarm me. Another flashback to frighten. I feel like I'm yet again engulfed in the quicksand that is TRAUMA. Where are you, God?" In all honesty, I felt like my FEELINGS OVERRODE MY FAITH. Even knowing all the while that doubting EVERYTHING is a common part of OVERWHELMING emotion. For me, these were times, truthfully, I needed a lifeline. We mustn't forget that GOD PLACES people and opportunities in our lives; take advantage of these resources. A call to my therapist, a small tweak in my medication, a visit with a dear friend, a reminder from my husband that *he IS AVAILABLE, AND A SAFE SPOT;* is needed in times such as this. I will be the first to say, that MY BIBLE IS my number one go-to for answers; *but when stumbling in fear that seems to block our view of even 'the GOOD', God gives us mercy in time of need.* (For we do not have a high priest who is unable to sympathize with our weakness, but one who in every respect has been tempted as we are, yet without sin. Let us then with confidence draw near to the throne of grace that we may receive mercy and find grace to help in time of need. Hebrews 4:15,16 ESV) I love that this high priest sympathizes with my weaknesses, He was tempted too; although HIS FAITH NEVER WAIVERED. Who better to PUT MY WEAK FAITH IN? "But blessed is the one who trusts in the Lord, whose confidence is in Him." Jeremiah 17:7 (ESV) As I trust in HIM and have CONFIDENCE IN HIM, this brings me HOPE in times of great need. And truly, when tumbling around for the hundredth time in wounds that are assumed long since healed, we NEED THIS HOPE! (Romans 15: 13 (ESV) May the God of hope fill you with all joy and peace in believing, so that by the power of the Holy Spirit you may abound in hope.) I love what scriptures like this share with me, I AM NOT IN CHARGE OF MUSTERING THIS 'JOY AND PEACE' when it seems entirely out of my capabilities in my state of *melt-down mode*. This is when, as Paul tells me, as a *BELIEVER*, the power of the Holy Spirit, through the GOD OF HOPE will fill me. This is the hope I need, not feelings of SHAME BECAUSE I CAN'T FEEL IT, I CAN'T DO IT...I just can't seem to KNOW IT! This is where I pray to My Heavenly Father for HIS strength, and HIS power; knowing in hope and faith, that HE will ONCE AGAIN RESTORE ME.

"There is surely a future hope for you, and your hope will not be cut off." Proverbs 23:18 ESV

"There is surely a future hope for you, and your hope will not be cut off."

Proverbs 23:18

What emotions need to be addressed in me right now? I understand it's time to stop ignoring them. Time to face them head-on. Holding God's hand; step in by faith to those emotions. Lord, what is my next step . . .

For I know the plans I have for you, declares the LORD, plans for welfare and not for evil, to give you a future and a hope.

Jeremiah 29:11

_____
_____
_____
_____
_____
_____
_____
_____
_____
_____
_____
_____
_____
_____

Do not be anxious about anything, but in everything by prayer and supplication with thanksgiving let your requests be made known to God. And the peace of God which surpasses all understanding will guard your hearts and minds in Christ Jesus.

Philippians 4:6,7

Thank you, God, for hearing and knowing my heart. Your peace gives me hope for my future. Amen.

Whatever Is Honorable

Choose to shine.

> Finally, brothers (sisters), whatever is true, whatever is honorable, whatever is just, whatever is pure, whatever is lovely, whatever is commendable, if there is any excellence, if there is anything worthy of praise, think about these things. What you have learned and received and heard and seen in me—*practice these things*, and the God of peace will be with you. Philippians 4:8-9 (ESV)

THIS IS WHERE IT IS TIME TO FOLLOW THROUGH WITH ALL THOSE HONORABLE, PURE, AND commendable thoughts. To 'put our money where our mouth is', so to speak! To *start PRACTICING them*, that is. If we want the peace that surpasses all understanding, GOD'S PEACE, we must put into practice His ways.

For me, I knew immediately what DIDN'T work in my life; what certainly had NOT been giving me this PEACE that God offered. I knew changing my thought patterns was entirely possible. I had worked many long years to dismantle, through God's VIEWPOINT, much Brainspotting, and EMDR, all that needed to be changed and REWIRED in my brain and body. If these were *out of sync* in my system and not aligning with God's Word, they should, through the power of the Holy Spirit be dismantled. (2 Corinthians 10:3-6 (ESV) For though we walk in the flesh, we are not waging war according to the flesh. For the weapons of our warfare are not of the flesh but have divine power to destroy strongholds. We destroy arguments and every lofty opinion raised against the knowledge of God, and take every thought captive to obey Christ, being ready to punish every disobedience, when your obedience is complete.) We know, here Paul is addressing the people of Corinth; those boasting their philosophical prowess; his was, by Divine Power, to capture their thoughts to obey CHRIST. This is all about obedience to Christ and right thinking towards CHRIST.

True today, *'smarts' alone will not DESTROY all that is faulty*, wired deeply in our brains without the HOLY SPIRIT doing this work through us. Seek God's face, open yourself whole-heartedly to be conformed to Christ's image. Reviewing what Paul also reminded the Corinthians in his previous letter, "The first man Adam became a living being": the last Adam (CHRIST) became a life-giving spirit. (1 Corinthians 15:45 ESV) Just as we have borne the image of the man of dust, we shall also bear the image of the man of heaven. (1 Corinthians 15:49 ESV) The LIFE-GIVING SPIRIT is ours through Christ's death on the cross. This is KEY, as this is what was needed and given: Christ's LIFE-GIVING SPIRIT.

As I meditated on all that is THIS LIFE-GIVING SPIRIT; the SPIRIT that dwells inside of me, I knew this obedience and 'right thinking' towards CHRIST should reach higher than the 'man of dust'. This 'right thinking' regarding Christ's IMAGE, living purposefully, living whole-heartedly in His image, alone gave me a peaceful mindset in which to approach the view of my behavior as a Christ Image-Bearer. Christ's life was one of obedience to His Father. His life was about the ultimate sacrifice. I contemplated putting all things honorable, commendable, pure, lovely, just, and true into place in my life in a more tangible way; a Jesus way of living. Following through the scripture…if there is anything worthy of praise, think about these things…my mind immediately took me to my friends. My friends that I was drawn to; that had taken up residence in my life and my heart. A friend whose son is the same age as my 23-year-old daughter, yet with his Down syndrome and Autism; could he be 5 years old, as he still, for the most part, is non-verbal? Once he was born, this dear woman turned her entire life upside down for this 5th child of hers. She continues to sacrifice her time and energy, always with a smile and miles of humility. This IS JESUS SACRIFICE. I thought of another close friend, a single mother, whose two children, now grown, were driven the 30-plus miles to attend our small Catholic School, for the 'EXTRA' that a faith-based education could afford her kids. Then back the 30 miles to take care of her aging parents, in the end, even having her Dad as her constant companion in her passenger's seat, until his death. All the while holding down multiple jobs. This is JESUS SACRIFICE. I recounted the long years that my Bible Study Ladies lovingly prayed and held me through the most difficult years of my life. The continual scripture that healed and propelled me forward in my long fight for freedom from complex PTSD and all that seemed to try and sink me. This is JESUS SACRIFICE. My husband and best friend; I thought of the hours he spent caring for me as I melted down, needing protection from haunting 'ghosts' of men in my past. A man *who showed me THE FATHER'S UNCONDITIONAL LOVE, this side of heaven.* This is JESUS SACRIFICE.

Suddenly I knew what I needed to do to live this HONORABLE life that I vowed to embark on. I would continue EXACTLY as I was! Foster these relationships; do life with the purest, most honorable people that the Lord (YAHWEH-JIREH…THE GOD WHO PROVIDES.) continually brought into my life. I would persist in learning by example as we loved and lived our authentic lives together. Those who BRING LIFE THROUGH THE SPIRIT LIVING INSIDE. I will follow their lead, being Christ Image-Bearers, as we all lead each other home. Thank you, Lord Jesus, for Your Sacrifice, and praise You, God, for those You have put in my path.

Our Sadness Shows Our Depth

You are bigger than your struggle.

THERE WERE TIMES THROUGH THE MANY YEARS OF RAISING MY CHILDREN WHEN I WOULD come across a mom that I would befriend who was different from the other moms. She seemed to have an 'old' soul, a far-away look in her eye, a wisdom to her words that would strike a chord in me. It would not be until a bit later that she would lead me to the core of her depth. After living a life of 'much' with my past revisited and my soul laid bare: I feel it is truly in our sadness that we gain depth and intense perception of not just ourselves but of others. We are then allowed to breathe greater compassion to all whom God brings into our path. And I do believe He brings those that need what our wounds have SHOWN US to help them through THEIR journey.

Sin wants to isolate us and pull us away from Our Lord's TRUTH. I found the dreadfulness and intensity that my traumatic memories recovered led to self-isolation and in turn that same pulling away from God's presence at times. Yet we mustn't forget in our suffering and sadness we have GAINED NEW DIMENSION of the knowledge of what God has done for us through our Savior Jesus Christ. We are saved because of this single act. Even Jesus cried out in SADNESS as he hung from that cross as *all OUR SIN was placed on HIM*, "My God, My God, why have You forsaken me?" (Matthew 27:46 ESV) But soon after, His reminder of the MEASURE OR DEPTH of what He had done for us in HIS LOVE. …And behold, "I am with you always, to the end of the age." Matthew 28:20 (ESV)

Working through the sadness of sin and the depravity of what was done to me as a small child wasn't easy. But as I read scripture and noticed even Jesus feeling forsaken, my Spirit seemed to encourage the feelings to come. I believe God wants us to process our feelings of deep pain, and betrayal; all of it needs to be laid at the feet of Jesus and brought before God. We mustn't hide it away for the ugliness it encompasses, assuming it will evaporate.

It doesn't. It takes on a life of its own and our futures are played out through the lens of these wounds, bleeding out of emotion in one way or another on all who engage us. God wants so much more for us. Releasing the HURT on days that I cried, "My God, My God, why?"… I heard whispered, "But I am with you until the end." Knowing I wasn't alone in my anguish, *Jesus was alongside me in my suffering, soothed as well as strengthened me in my fight for freedom.* I PRAISE YOU JESUS, FOR YOUR SACRIFICE!

With God & Through God...I Am Bigger Than My Struggle.

Have I let my trauma lead me to self-isolation? I mustn't let this pull me away from my relationship with God. Through my suffering and sadness, does this give me an increased knowledge of what God has done for me through my Savior Jesus Christ? Am I encouraging my feelings to come? Remember, hiding them is NOT the answer; God wants more for me. Am I constantly reminding myself I am not alone in my healing? Jesus is with me always.

_____
_____
_____
_____
_____
_____
_____
_____
_____
_____
_____
_____
_____
_____
_____
_____
_____

BE STILL AND KNOW

Wait for the Lord.

LEARNING...OR WOULD IT BE TRUSTING GOD IN THE CORE OF WHO I AM; THAT I HAVE VALUE seemed a tall ask. Characteristic of the swirling ugly that wants to overtake survivors of trauma when triggers are a part of our recovery, make 'feeling good' about ourselves quite tenuous. As much as we want to claim the resilience all others see in our character, we struggle to lay claim to our internal sense of value because of what was done to us. Those triggers were met with much therapy, some likened me to a 'masochist'...*AS IF one would enjoy repeated therapies to alleviate triggers.* YES, it was difficult, tedious, and painful, BUT as triggers lessened and horrific somatic symptoms were relieved, I knew therapy was a GODSEND.

Possibly, the one aspect of EMDR and the methods of therapies used to help me lay hold to my past and reclaim my life that I might have changed would be the *'race to the finish line'.* So eager to be DONE, I pushed and prodded and exhausted myself. The adage, "No rest for the weary," was certainly my mantra for the entire first year. I believe I did my body, my nervous system, and my poor family a disservice; we were all thoroughly depleted. Seeing now...IT TAKES AS LONG AS IT TAKES!

I think trauma, or maybe is it just life in general, has convinced us that we can't or shouldn't take time to rest. We don't have to EARN REST; it is NOT A REWARD to be given only after a grueling day! We forget that *God gave us that all-important rest for OUR betterment and OUR well-being*...and not JUST on that seventh day. I think HE WAS MAKING A POINT; no doubt HE could have continued HIS CREATING for days ON END!

And on the seventh day, God finished His work that He had done, and He rested on the seventh day from all His work that He had done. So God blessed the seventh day and made it holy, because on it God rested from all His work that He had done in creation. Genesis 2:2,3 (ESV)

"Come to me, all you who are weary and burdened, and I will give you rest. Take my yoke upon you and learn from me, for I am gentle and humble in heart, and you will find rest for your souls. For my yoke is easy and my burden is light." Matthew 11:28-30 (ESV)

The apostles returned to Jesus and told Him all that they had done and taught. And He said to them, "Come away by yourselves to a desolate (quiet) place and rest awhile." For many were coming and going, and they had no leisure even to eat. Mark 6:30,31 (ESV)

In Psalms 23:1-4 (ESV) The LORD is my shepherd; I shall not want. He makes me lie down in green pastures. He leads me beside still waters. He restores my soul. He leads me in paths of righteousness for His name's sake. Even though I walk through the valley of the shadow of death, I will fear no evil, for you are with me your rod and your staff, they comfort me…God not only encourages us to rest, but HE also leads us to those still waters and MAKES US REST, so He can restore our souls and strengthen us for what lies ahead.

As the hard work of healing turned into years, I started realizing just how important rest was to my mind as well as my nervous system. In verses such as Psalm 46, I found encouragement for my soul as well. Knowing that amid confusion and turmoil, not only do we need to take time to 'rest' and 'be still' but to *enjoy the PEACE of God's presence.* God also commands us to 'stop fighting' and 'stop striving' and realize WHO is on our side through our conflicts, strife, and struggles. In doing so we can hope to find comfort in the chaos. Being STILL (Or as the original Hebrew root tells us "Let Go.") is not always easy for those who have lived lives of striving. Just as the Israelites were called to recognize that the LORD was with them in their battles, we too must believe GOD WILL fight our battles (big and small) and we need to allow it by LETTING GO and getting out of His way.

Psalm 46:1-10 (ESV) God is our REFUGE and STRENGTH, A VERY PRESENT HELP in trouble. Therefore, WE WILL NOT FEAR though the earth gives way, though the mountains be moved into the heart of the sea, though its waters roar and foam, though the mountains tremble at its swelling. There is a river whose streams make glad the city of God, the holy habitation of the Most High. GOD IS IN THE MIDST OF HER; SHE SHALL NOT BE MOVED; GOD WILL HELP HER when morning dawns. The nations rage, the kingdoms totter; He utters His voice, and the earth melts. The LORD OF HOSTS

IS WITH US; the God of Jacob is OUR FORTRESS. Come, behold the works of the LORD, how he has brought desolations on the earth. He makes wars cease to the end of the earth; he breaks the bow and shatters the spear; He burns the chariots with fire. "BE STILL AND KNOW THAT I AM GOD. I WILL BE EXALTED AMONG THE NATIONS; I WILL BE EXALTED IN THE EARTH!"

AMEN TO THAT! Forgetting we are NOT God; we are NOT IN CONTROL is mighty freeing. There is much WAITING ON GOD, much RESTING IN GOD during the healing of trauma wounds, we are called to 'wait on the LORD', and applying this as we continue our healing and continue life seems difficult. But with God, there is ALWAYS A WAY.

Psalm 27:14 (ESV) Wait for the LORD; be strong and take heart and wait for the LORD. AMEN.

REST IN HIM…HE RESTORES. HE ENCOURAGES. HE LEADS US TO STILL WATERS…LET GO.

It seems the dreadfulness of our past, sins, and failures want to lead us to self isolation, in turn, maybe even isolation from God. Remember, Jesus felt very much alone ("My God, My God, why have You forsaken me?") as He hung on the cross taking all our sins upon himself. Jesus, help me welcome and release my feelings. What do I need to let go of to encourage healing?

_____
_____
_____
_____
_____
_____
_____
_____
_____
_____
_____
_____
_____
_____
_____
_____
_____

"Come to me, all who labor and are heavy laden, and I will give you rest. Take my yoke upon you, and learn from me, for I am gentle and lowly in heart, and you will find rest for your souls. For my yoke is easy and my burden is light."

Matthew 11:28-30

Honesty Is Acceptance

Peace beyond understanding.

I claim to be nothing if not honest, almost to a fault. Shopping with my daughters could be problematic. "What do you think of this, Mom?" The answer was not always ideal. I just COULD NOT answer any other way BUT HONESTLY; at times hurting tender feelings possibly. If there is one thing that I have instilled in my children is, "Be honest above all else." Lying was NOT PERMITTED in our house. This is not to say that my teenagers would not, on occasion, use the fine art of omission. Neglecting to share ALL details to skirt the truth at times, but in the end, the truth seemed to win out.

As I have recovered memories, from parts of my childhood that I had SUPPRESSED, and have had to deal with the dishonesty of what others have done to me, my sense of equilibrium has been thrown off-kilter. I have experienced lying before from a loved one, but even then, I seemed to understand the self-preservation mode one gets themselves into. One lie will often lead to the next, and so on and so on. Not that I excused it, but I think as an adult I was able to process it. However, the deception and cruelty that was done to me as a child before coping mechanisms were in place were much more detrimental to my sense of survival. *Even my much older mind struggled to be honest with myself at times to accept all that I knew happened. Until we honestly accept our stormy past can we move forward in our process.* EVEN THEN, moving forward to accept what happened, I struggled to understand how men/boys could be so dreadful and do such heinous acts. Finally, I realized that to come to a place of acceptance and a place of PEACE that goes beyond all understanding, I had to 'give up' my RIGHT TO UNDERSTAND any of the actions that were done. I could not understand any of it. HONESTLY, I HAD TO LEAVE IT ALL AT THE FEET OF JESUS. *THERE I FOUND ACCEPTANCE AS WELL AS PEACE.*

FINDING PEACE

I HAVE COME TO A PLACE OF ACCEPTANCE AND A PLACE OF PEACE THAT GOES BEYOND ALL UNDERSTANDING . I HAVE TO 'GIVE UP' MY RIGHT TO UNDERSTAND ANY  OF THE ACTIONS THAT WERE DONE TO ME. IT IS DIFFICULT TO UNDERSTAND ANY OF IT. HONESTLY, I HAD TO LEAVE IT ALL AT THE FEET OF JESUS. THERE I FOUND ACCEPTANCE AS WELL AS PEACE.

As I have been working through my process of acknowledging, acceptance, forgiving, and moving forward; how do I feel my progression and growth are unfolding?

_____
_____
_____
_____
_____
_____
_____
_____
_____
_____
_____
_____

I Am Fierce

I have persevered.

THE MORE I STUDIED THE BIBLE AND ESPECIALLY THE GOSPELS THE MORE I CAME TO realize that the GOOD NEWS of the GOSPEL IS for the brokenhearted. This seemed a revelation to me, at some point, as I'd focused ONLY on the STRENGTH of many characters in this important book; I'd overlooked much. Not grasping the fact; we are to look at these characters of the Old Testament, (Referred to throughout the Bible: the Old as well as the New Testament) not as MODELS for our lives but as MIRRORS: from the powerful Abraham, ready to sacrifice his son at but a request from HIS HOLY GOD, or Moses leading the Israelites out of Egypt after all those years in exile, or David, the man after GOD'S OWN HEART. As I studied these characters and so many more; I realized that there was MUCH that led these powerful men to be able to have the fierce faith and strength to pursue such greatness.

Abraham had many *shortcomings, failings, and flaws which ALL LED to the fervency of his faith.* Moses' life of MUCH found him murdering a man as he stood up for God's chosen people, yet God placed him in the position of leadership *despite his SIN.* While David was King, his total lapse in judgment and/or faith led him to murder a man for purely selfish reasons; to steal this man's wife for his own. David's repentance took months and a confrontation with the Prophet Nathan. *Confession of his sin to the Lord* and asking for forgiveness began repentance in his life, even giving all that he owned, before his death, to build God's Holy Temple.

These, like so many stories in the Bible show the FIERCENESS of character one must have to persevere. Despite our best efforts, this fallen world we live in tries to hold us in chains. My struggle from the pit of self-discovery to health held me in those chains for quite some time. I think, just where Satan wants us. Believing all those lies we bought into: 'God could never love someone like us, we could never be good enough, or clean enough.' NOT TRUE. We must FIERCELY fight through the blanket of lies Satan wants to hold over us. FIERCELY struggle to release the character God created in us that had been dormant, waiting to be freed. As Charles H. Spurgeon is quoted, "If the service of God is worth anything, it is worth everything,"

A favorite quote from my sweet husband that I hold onto, on those all too frequent times, when I fail in my walk with God is, "This is not out of a lack of SPIRITUALITY *but out of a sign of my HUMANITY.*"

Thank you, LORD, for the humility to realize and accept my humanity as You lead me in my walk with You. AMEN.

We must **FIERCELY** fight through the blanket of lies Satan wants to hold over us.

FIERCELY struggle to release the character God created in us that has been dormant, waiting to be freed.

As we fight and struggle through recovery we have times of failure. Remember, this is not out of a lack of Spirituality but out of a sign of our Humanity.

Thank you, Lord, for the humility to realize and accept my humanity as You lead me in my walk with You. Amen.

BREATHE HIM IN

Exhale your past.

BE STILL AND KNOW. IRONICALLY, THOSE OF US MESSED WITH IN THE WORST OF WAYS; we've lived our lives in a type of chaos, confusion, as well a tremendous state of shame. As we heal, being still, breathing in God's love, and His living presence, and knowing He loves us is a DIFFICULT endeavor. I found that even taking a deep breath was almost an impossible ask. It was DEEP INTO MY HEALING, when I walked into my therapist's office, sat on his loveseat, and shocked him with the statement, *"I can finally take a deep breath."* For the first time in many years, I was relaxed enough to breathe in a life-sustaining deep breath as opposed to the short, shallow breaths that tended to keep my body in fight, flight, or freeze mode. For those of us who have never really *felt SAFE*, AT EASE, OR COMFORTABLE *in our skin*, well, you get this. We find ourselves in a constant state of turmoil, barely surviving life, and certainly living with instability and skewed beliefs about our identity. In opposition, the 'SAFETY' of breathing in God's love and being healthy enough to acknowledge this in our core, IS A HUGE BREAKTHROUGH for us.

We are to BELIEVE the 'TRUTH' of what God says about us. But for those of us who have bodies that have harbored feelings for years of violence and abuse, which in turn led to the emotional negative wiring of our brains; we struggle. Our 'WIRED TRUTH' certainly has done a number on us. The rewiring takes time, energy, and God's enduring GRACE. That moment of BREATHING HIM IN, finally feeling safe enough to relax my tense body enough to take that glorious deep breath of life, my SPIRIT SOARED. I knew at that moment that I was closer than I'd EVER BEEN to feeling this ONENESS with GOD'S SPIRIT; this breathing in of stillness and life; God's PEACE.

The Spirit of God has made me, and the breath of the Almighty gives me life. Job 33:4 (ESV)

I will INHALE THE FUTURE AND EXHALE THE PAST; PRAISE GOD for Your healing and YOUR BREATH OF LIFE IN MY LUNGS!

THE SPIRIT OF GOD HAS MADE ME, AND THE BREATH OF THE ALMIGHTY GIVES ME LIFE.
JOB 33:4

I WILL INHALE THE FUTURE AND EXHALE THE PAST: PRAISE GOD FOR YOUR HEALING AND YOUR BREATH OF LIFE IN MY LUNGS!

GET TO KNOW GOD

See the possibilities!

KNOWING GOD WELL IS TRANSFORMATIONAL. THE MORE I READ GOD'S WORD THROUGH scripture the more I was (and am) learning who He is. Getting to know God through time spent deepening my understanding of Him, the more I see how this knowledge of HIS character is changing me. God designed us for deep communion with Him. Quiet time in His Presence is transforming me into who He created me to be—deeply tied to HIS ACCEPTANCE AND HIS LOVE. Knowing this frees us to live our lives allowing that love and mercy to flow out of us. Knowing the peace and joy that only comes from HIS ACCEPTANCE; that of which, I had searched, like many, to find in externally validating means.

How many times in my life, have I trudged through, *working to gain favor* in my strength, looking for the validation that, as a youngster seemed to be lacking? Now, knowing my search and work have come to a screeching halt. I wonder, far more often than I should, what is the learning curve like, for those who have not experienced boatloads of trauma to their younger selves. Did they inherently know better, unlike me, 'there is no need to make life about *constant perfection*?' Does their 'call' from God come peacefully as opposed to our long hard fight; which I compared to much in our life: BEING a fight? SALVATION, GRACE, AND MERCY…"God, how can this be given freely without me battling as I have always done in my life? Where is the catch here? This Peace, this Mercy, and Grace…what needs to be done for YOU TO TRULY ACCEPT ME?"

2 Thessalonians 3:16 (ESV) Now may the Lord of PEACE HIMSELF give you PEACE at all times and in every way. The Lord be with you ALL.

So, we are ALWAYS enveloped in HIS PEACE, which is inherent in God's PRESENCE! GOD'S PRESENCE is beyond my understanding, so stop using my measly mindset to try and comprehend this; BE STILL and INVITE GOD INTO MY SPACE INSTEAD, always looking to HIM for HIS PEACE. Certainly, the world and my ways have failed me, yet I am discovering GOD NEVER DOES.

Now may the Lord of PEACE HIMSELF give you PEACE at all times and in every way. The Lord be with you ALL.

2 Thessalonians 3:16

Knowing God well is Transformational. As I spend time in communion with God... How has this changed, not only the love and acceptance I feel from God, but how freely it pours out of me? _____
_____
_____
_____
_____
_____
_____
_____
_____
_____
_____
_____
_____
_____
_____
_____
_____
_____
_____
_____

Am I leaving behind the need for external validation & laying aside working for constant perfection? _____
_____
_____

PATIENCE IN THE BECOMING

Some wake up to an alarm, others wake up to a Calling.

I THINK THERE IS A POINT IN EVERYONE'S LIFE WHEN WE REALIZE WE COME TO A crossroads. There is a fork in the road, and we have a choice to make. For many it is life-altering. Do I continue as I have, assuming this is how my life is meant to be OR do I listen to this urging either small or in my case, screaming at me of change on the horizon? *Change IS alarming*; it can be catastrophic, or rejuvenating, but IT NO DOUBT WILL BE WEIGHTY. I discovered that much time and energy may well be spent *focusing on fighting* and *THEN accepting* the change occurring. Whether they be OLD MEMORIES, old habits, stale relationships, or lives that bring us no joy: these changes must be dealt with before we can even begin to build on the NEW. PATIENCE IS KEY as *we must first UNBECOME* all that has been layered on us…BEFORE WE CAN BECOME THIS NEW CREATION. A creation that yearns for connection with each other. We must replace our insecurities and anxieties with confidence and strength that only comes from the Grace of God within. I truly believe that is where the fork of the road is leading: Time to lean into this BEAUTIFUL GRACE OF GOD. Unlearn old habits of self-serving, self-importance, self-centeredness, and extreme self-reliance. It is time to move into an open-handed flow of giving GRACE to others that only comes from accessing that SPIRIT. This pure HEART-FELT GRACE only comes from this *renewal* of our SPIRIT WITHIN US.

Create in me a pure heart, O God, and renew a steadfast spirit within me. Psalms 51:10 (ESV)

UNBECOMING

Maybe the Journey
isn't so much about becoming anything . . .
Maybe it's about
unbecoming
everything that isn't
really you,
So you can be
who you were
meant to be in the
first place.

Paulo Coelho

His Enduring Grace

"But the Lord stood with me and strengthened me."
2 Timothy 4:1 ESV

LOOKING BACK FOR ME MUST BE A FLEETING GLANCE: I MUSTN'T SPEND EXCESSIVE TIME in the terribly painful parts of my past. Yet, I love that I can now take note of God's abounding love that He showered on me throughout my life. (Remember NOT the former things, nor consider the things of OLD. Behold I am doing a NEW thing; now it springs forth, do you not perceive it? I will make a way in the wilderness and rivers in the desert. Isaiah 43:18,19 ESV) The withholding of dreadful memories *'until a time such as this'* that I could devote to processing and healing such wounds—a time when my eight children were mostly independent. The initial veil placed, in the form of dissociation, allowed me to have my children; this certainly was a freedom I might not have ALLOWED myself due to the traumatic memories. And probably the biggest blessing is raising my children without the dreadful FEAR that I have lived in as I've discovered and processed such violence.

I had lived a life unwittingly built on the lies of shame and unworthiness of my past. Believing I must earn the love of God; but as I recount all the ways God was showing such perpetual, relentless, unfailing steady devotion to me, HOW, I wonder now, could I have ever doubted HIS ENDURING LOVE AND GRACE?

Isaiah 41:10 (ESV) Fear not, for I am with you; be not dismayed, for I am your God; I will strengthen you, I will help you, I will uphold you with My righteous right hand.

This enduring GRACE which God has been showering on me steadily as I have, oh-so-slowly, been learning what the Lord's been teaching: HE WILL KEEP SUSTAINING ME, HE WILL KEEP BLESSING ME, AND HE WILL KEEP LOVING ME. This is where we must quit resisting God: We must take the *RESTORATION through GRACE* that God freely offers.

Remember not the former things, nor consider the things of old. Behold I am doing a new thing; now it springs forth, do you not perceive it? I will make a way in the wilderness and rivers in the desert..

Isaiah 43:18.19

Am I believing that God is doing a 'new thing' in my life? Here is where I must count my blessings of the past and know God 'makes a way in the wilderness'. Listing these might help... _____

_____

_____

_____

GOD'S MASTERPIECE

Be the unique and beautiful you that God called you to be.

WE JOKE ABOUT CREATING A "MASTERPIECE"; THOSE OF US WHO ARE 'ARTSY'. A WORK of art we are proud of; something we call our own, that much time, thought, and effort was crafted into this piece of beauty. It is very PERSONAL to us. It holds SPECIAL MEANING IN OUR HEART, NO DOUBT.

Truly WE are considered GOD'S MASTERPIECES. "For we are God's masterpiece. He has created us anew in Christ Jesus, so we can do the good things He planned for us long ago." (Ephesians 2:10 NLT)

As I had spent the better part of my life living in a state of unworthiness and shame; not recognizing much of God's glory due to '*feelings of brokenness*', my reflection of God's love for me had me questioning how much effort God had put into this piece of 'artwork--me'. Here is where wrangling those thoughts came into play. Applying GOD'S truth to the lies I had lived in for so many years.

Ephesians 3:17-19 (ESV) And I pray that you, being rooted and established in love, may have power, together with the Lord's holy people, to grasp how wide and long and high and deep is the love of Christ, and to know this love that surpasses knowledge—that you may be filled to the measure of God.

1 John 3:1 (ESV) See what kind of love the Father has given to us, that we should be called children of God, and so we are. The reason why the world does not know us is that it did not know Him. Psalm 136:26 (ESV) Give thanks to God of heaven, for His steadfast love endures forever.

Isaiah 54:10 ESV) "Though the mountains be shaken, and the hills be removed, yet my unfailing love for you will not be shaken nor my covenant of peace be removed," says the Lord, who has compassion on you.

Lamentations 3:22,23 (ESV) The steadfast love of the LORD never ceases; His mercies never come to an end; they are new every morning; great is Your faithfulness. Lamentations 3:32,33 (NIV) Though He brings grief, He will show compassion, so great is His unfailing love. For He does not willingly bring affliction or grief to anyone.

Now that I have all these PROMISES OF GOD'S LOVE for me, I am feeling, and BELIEVING I AM THIS MASTERPIECE OF GOD'S: What a tremendous gift. A well-thought-out creation, meticulously made, crafted as a thing of beauty and splendor, of which God is PROUD. I praise YOU, for I am fearfully and wonderfully made. Wonderful are Your works; my soul knows it very well. Psalm 139:14 (ESV)

"For we are God's masterpiece.
He has created us anew in Christ
Jesus, so we can do the good things
He planned for us long ago."

Ephesians 2:10

I am created in His image and I am God's Masterpiece! My attributes are...

HIS POWER IS MY STRENGTH

As I remain fierce but flexible

THE DAY I REALIZED I WAS NOT ALONE IN MY HEALING WAS THE DAY I BELIEVED I COULD BE 'FIXED'. The day Matt, my therapist, helped me discover my childhood sexual abuse that had simmered for years causing a plethora of mental and physical issues. Knowing you are supported, you can 'get' strength from another, and that you are *NOT ALONE IN YOUR FIGHT* is monumental. Being dissociated from our past, ignoring the reality of pain inflicted, or just living a life scattering the hurt and damaged parts of ourselves to those around us seems 'normal'. Yet we know deep down inside ourselves something is amiss. God called me to something MORE in a 'big way'. We will call it a 'breakdown'. A time for a BIG CHANGE was in my future.

As we finally begin to open ourselves up to the help and support of OTHERS, I believe our hearts are ignited; the *ALONENESS* that we had lived a lifetime in, melts away, and we are in a community, with not just loving allies but champions for the cause. They cheer for our victories and cry with us as they hold us up on our tough days. I was suddenly understanding that 'THE CHURCH' that Paul talks of in Ephesians 2:18-22 (ESV) For through Him [Jesus] we both have access in one Spirit to the Father. So then you are no longer strangers and aliens, but you are fellow citizens with the saints and members of the household of God, built on the foundation of the apostles and prophets, Christ Jesus himself being the cornerstone, in whom the whole structure, being joined [interconnected] together grows [rises] into a holy temple in the Lord. In Him, you also are being built together into a dwelling place for God by the Spirit.

I was FEELING this *interconnectedness* and this rising, a soaring of sorts to new heights in my faith. I was not ALONE, neither an alien in my body nor my space on Earth. I fit into this 'BODY OF CHRIST' in a powerful way. With a foundation so indestructible, so 'rock solid' I was free to be who God created me to be. This strength was something I could not possess ALONE, or certainly sustain for long periods throughout my life, BUT IN COMMUNITY, WITH CHRIST as our main focus, we were STRONG.

Psalm 59:16 (ESV) But I will sing of Your strength; I will sing aloud of Your steadfast love in the morning, For you have been to me a fortress and a refuge in the day of my distress.

Psalm 59:17 (ESV) O my strength, I will sing praises to You, for You, O God, are my fortress, the God who shows me steadfast love.

Psalm 61:2b,3 (ESV) Lead me to the rock that is higher than I, for You have been my refuge, a strong tower against the enemy.

Psalm 62:8 (ESV) Trust in Him at all times, o people; pour out your heart before Him; God is a refuge for us.

Isaiah 40:26b (ERSV) …by the greatness of His might and because He is strong in power, not one is missing.

Isaiah 40:29 (ESV) He gives power to the faint, and to him who has no might He increases strength.

Isaiah 41:10 (ESV) Fear not, for I am with you; be not dismayed, for I am your God; I will strengthen you, I will help you, I will uphold you with my righteous right hand.

We do ourselves a disservice by living in our strength, afraid to reach out to others and Our Father. It seemed the weaker I felt, *the stronger my 'church' held me*, and the tighter God's hold; the stronger His Presence felt. God, YOU truly are my fortress, my strong tower, and my REFUGE. Praise God for the community of believers; through their many BLESSINGS, God's heart is made manifest.

HIS POWER IS MY STRENGTH

We are stronger in a 'community' of believers.

For through Him [Jesus] we both have access in one Spirit to the Father. So then you are no longer strangers and aliens, but you are fellow citizens with the saints and members of the household of God, built on the foundation of the apostles and prophets, Christ Jesus Himself being the cornerstone, in whom the whole structure, being joined together grows into a holy temple in the Lord. In Him, you also are being built together into a dwelling place for God by the Spirit.
Ephesians 2:18-22

Who does 'My Church' consist of? Am I noticing God's Presence enveloping me as my people support me? Am I remembering to praise Him for Blessing me with the strength to persevere?

_____
_____
_____
_____
_____
_____
_____
_____
_____
_____

Fear not, for I am with you; be not dismayed, for I am your God; I will strengthen you, I will help you, I will uphold you with my righteous right hand.   Isaiah 41:10

He gives power to the faint, and to him who has no might He increases strength.
Isaiah 40:29

THE BLESSING OF WOMANHOOD

So very thankful

THE THRILL OF BEING GIVEN 2 SONS AND 6 DAUGHTERS, A GIFT FROM GOD. AS IF HE WAS telling me, "You've got this, this mothering thing, and these children, they are here for you to teach them the way to go." I LOVED MOTHERING. I have loved the part of having a baby, feeding, cooing, holding, and even diapering this little sweet soul God chose to entrust to me...TO ME! So, I could raise this child to follow in His ways. I could raise the world's next generation of Christ followers. *A BIG JOB*...but I was SO up for the challenge. Grandchildren as well, loving and more loving as only a grandparent can take the time to shower upon a grandchild; speaking love and positivity into this little being that is ready to absorb all that is being said to THEM AND ABOUT THEM. NO WORTHLESS MANTLES TO BE DUMPED by Grammys carrying theirs to haunt littles' dreams.

I believe that for me, being a woman brought many demands my way. But truly none that I didn't embrace. My first husband's meager salary taught me to count my pennies and much about living a life of frugality. Being left for another woman, and with my four children counting on me, suddenly God filled me with power, stamina, and determination *I CERTAINLY DID NOT KNOW I POSSESSED*. The prospects of a new husband; my *hope* soared...I absolutely knew God intended me to have more children with this new husband; my contentment seemed complete. But I believe there is ALWAYS A 'BUT' when we are looking for a person or a situation to meet all of our needs and we are living our lives in this place of 'total and complete contentment'...this side of heaven, anyway!

Marrying Geno meant learning to curb my tongue, living the life of a doctor's wife meant many eyes upon me. And how could that be a bad thing? I had always, ALWAYS been very vocal on all fronts. But my behavior was suddenly under the microscope. What started as a chance to dictate a 'new and improved' life turned into a heavy mantle to wear. *Measuring every word and action, it turns out does not free one to live a life of true freedom.*

To be FREE AND UNIQUE in the skin God put me in, meant a total shedding of all that was me. This included a deep dive into my past that rocked me to my very core. Finding what was hidden under the façade that I had created was exhausting. The walls and barriers around our hearts must be broken if we are to find ourselves; whom we are called to be in Christ. God does not want us just muddling through life, praying we will make it, and keeping ourselves busy from one day to the next. He never intended our emotions to be pushed to the pit of our bellies or the furthest reaches of our brains, cataloged far behind the to-do list of the day, simmering, awaiting the ulcer or the breakdown.

For me, much introspection was needed for God to shine His light on areas that needed healing. Do we even realize the remarks that fly at us as children that we internalize and hold tight, only to discover years later we are still browbeating ourselves over these? Do we see ourselves wanting, just NOT QUITE 'MEASURING UP', and *forever chasing PERFECTION* in everything from our bodies to our performance? Would the praise and affirmation BE ENOUGH at this point in our lives? Would we feel whole, complete, satisfied, peaceful, and full of freedom? BUT…how long would that last? For me, I realized I still felt small and insignificant…it is ONLY IN GOD'S LOVE that we find wholeness, acceptance, true LOVE, and true PEACE.

Psalm 73:26 (ESV) My flesh and my heart may fail, BUT GOD is the strength of my heart and my portion forever.

Psalm 119:45 (ESV) "I will walk about in freedom, for I have sought out Your precepts."

SOUL WOUNDS

Release it, to receive.

I REALIZED THE DEEP, DEEP SOUL WOUNDS RECEIVED ALONG MY LIFE'S JOURNEY NEEDED intentional mending if I was to continue in this 'walk in freedom'. For me, forgiveness was given, as I was called to do, but was there more? Leaning on God means listening to His urgings. More than just listening to God's word, it is pushing yourself to heed His call, even when, ESPECIALLY I suppose, when we want to run in the opposite direction. God urged me to push beyond the boundaries I had erected for myself during the early stages of healing. The complexity of healing our body, our mind, and our SOUL is a huge undertaking. There was much to be healed in God's loving plan for me, and I found it needed to be done in stages. This unfolding, I see now in retrospect, as the lovely plan of a gloriously LOVING FATHER.

These deep soul wounds that seemed to cling to me inhibited TOTAL healing. The abandonment issues, rejection, betrayal--the injustice of it all seemed to continue to hold me in a place of limbo. Not quite allowing me the freedom I knew God wanted for me. Complete healing is a total wholeness; seeing with 'Christ' eyes, not through 'fleshly' eyes which disrupts our relationship with God. If we are still struggling with any relationship— it affects our relationship with God. If we are laying our hurts, our wounds, and our pain from our past at Jesus' feet, this means our EVERYTHING. We cannot pick and choose what we cling to and what we release, *even if it is inadvertently*.

Jesus' ministry was a LOVE for everyone...EVERYONE: *Those broken by the world AND those DOING THE BREAKING*. Luke 6:19 (ESV) And all the crowd sought to touch Him, for power came out from Him and healed them ALL. "But I say to you who hear, love your enemies, do good to those who hate you, bless those who curse you, pray for those who abuse you." Luke 6:27,28 (ESV)

"And as you wish that others would do to you, do so to them." Luke 6:31 (ESV) "This is my commandment, that you love one another as I loved you." John 15:12 (ESV)

Loving as we define love is so flat when compared to the Hebrew definition. Throughout the Hebrew Bible, it is translated in any number of ways; steadfast love, mercy, kindness, and goodness… even firm. In Greek, the word for love is AGAPE, love between persons, or people of God, of God for humanity, and of God for Christ. *Agape love is founded upon deep appreciation and high regard, it is the love that God commands.*

Now was the time, I realized, to go deeper into this 'AGAPE LOVE' for those whom I, indeed felt deep soul wounds still lingered. Can I say it was easy? Can I say I desire this? I can say God desires this of me, and I can say I am here to answer to Him. And I do want to believe this wonderful Father of mine understands that for me, loving at a distance is the best way I can love some people.

I believe this *AGAPE LOVE* God wants in this world, once again, holds us to a higher standard. A standard that at times we feel, and think is impossible to live up to. AND, left to our own devices it IS IMPOSSIBLE! But through Christ within everything is possible.

Beloved, let us love one another, for love is from God, and whoever loves has been born of God and knows God. 1 John 4:7 (ESV)

QUEST FOR IDENTITY

Be unafraid to wake up and try.

MY SEARCH FOR THE 'TRUE ME' BEGAN IN EARNEST ONCE THE STRIPPING AWAY OF LAYER upon layer of my 'seedy' past surfaced, *was accepted*, and processed. This lengthy process of cutting away all that was scratchy, and abrasive left me raw. A new curiosity about WHO I WAS at the core of my being took over.

1 Corinthians 6:19,20 (ESV) Do you know that your bodies are temples of the Holy Spirit, who is in you, whom you received from God? You are not your own; you were bought at a price. Therefore, honor God with your bodies.

'You are not your own…HONOR GOD WITH YOUR BODY.' Here was where I fought my mind for control! It was certainly TRUE, I indeed felt that this body, at times was NOT MINE…I didn't want all that it contained; the *YUCK of my past had left quite a mark*. I certainly wanted to 'HONOR GOD WITH MY BODY'. Here is where we must ALWAYS remember WHO is in us; WHOM WE RECEIVED FROM GOD, and that we were bought at a very, very high price! Our bodies are TEMPLES. As I studied all there was about Solomon's building of God's Holy Temple in 1 Kings 5-7 (ESV); all that was 'shiny and bright' led me right back to where God TRULY DWELLS…in our hearts, our souls, our very beings, thanks to Jesus' sacrifice of His death on the CROSS: there is yet more freedom from this earthly body.

Galatians 3:27,28 (ESV) …for all of you who were baptized into Christ have clothed yourself with Christ. There is neither Jew nor Gentile, neither slave nor free, nor is there male and female, for you are all one in Christ Jesus.

1 Corinthians 12:27 (ESV) Now you are the body of Christ, and each one of you is a part of it.

My new IDENTITY, I suddenly realized, had NOTHING to do with what was done to my body in the past and EVERYTHING to do with what Jesus DID FOR ME. I was a member of Christ's body, clothed in His robes of SALVATION. This new robe felt nothing like the scratchy and abrasive wool coat I could never seem to shed until I took this freedom freely offered.

Searching for the 'TRUE ME'

C

A curious pattern

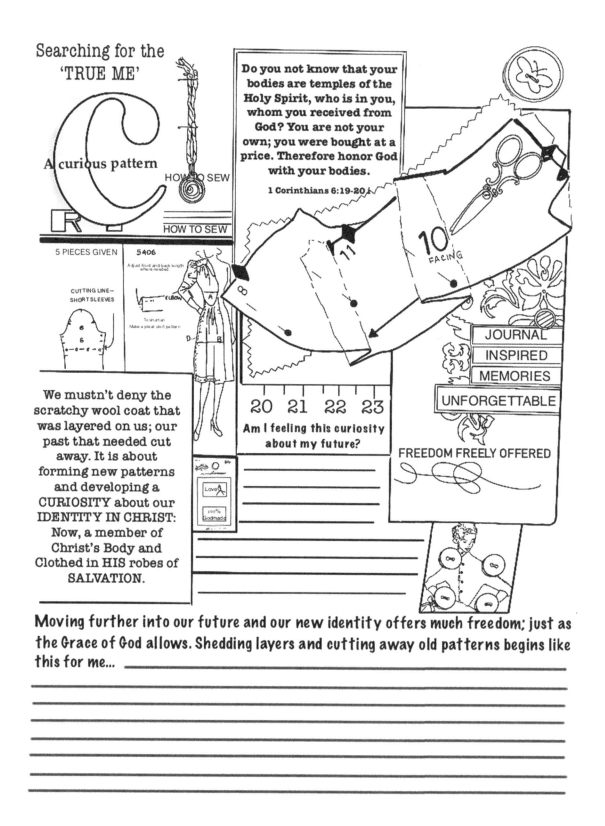

HOW TO SEW

HOW TO SEW

5 PIECES GIVEN   5406

CUTTING LINE—
SHORT SLEEVES

Do you not know that your bodies are temples of the Holy Spirit, who is in you, whom you received from God? You are not your own; you were bought at a price. Therefore honor God with your bodies.

1 Corinthians 6:19-20

10 FACING

11

8

20 21 22 23

Am I feeling this curiosity about my future?

JOURNAL

INSPIRED

MEMORIES

UNFORGETTABLE

FREEDOM FREELY OFFERED

We mustn't deny the scratchy wool coat that was layered on us; our past that needed cut away. It is about forming new patterns and developing a CURIOSITY about our IDENTITY IN CHRIST: Now, a member of Christ's Body and Clothed in HIS robes of SALVATION.

Moving further into our future and our new identity offers much freedom; just as the Grace of God allows. Shedding layers and cutting away old patterns begins like this for me...

_____

_____

_____

_____

_____

_____

_____

It's All About Jesus

Happenings and holy healing

I REALIZED THE MORE I SURRENDERED TO THIS WAY OF THINKING: I AM A MEMBER OF Christ's body, and it is ALL ABOUT JESUS! It is NOT about the 'happenings' of my life. It is not about the 'work' I put into being a member of Christ's body any more than it is in all the 'nasty' acts that were *perpetrated on my body* as a youngster, or during times I 'acted out' in my *ugly wounds*. And this was not trying to OUTTHINK surrendering as I had done before.

I believe there is a point in our healing process where we have truly worked through the ugly discovery of all the 'dirty and darkness' that NEEDED to be dealt with, wept for, and indeed processed our past. Wouldn't God want these bodies to be filled with all the light and beauty and knowledge of Himself as possible? I felt as the darkness was expelled so much space was left to be filled. Much space for all that is CHRIST WITHIN. Suddenly, it wasn't even about a decision made, for me, it was truly a feeling that I felt. How long had I waited for THIS? *An internal light that switched on*; so radically felt, I knew my life would NEVER be the same.

Hebrews 10:19-22 (ESV) "Therefore, brothers and sisters, since we have the confidence to enter the Most Holy Place by the blood of Jesus…let us draw near to God with a sincere heart and with the full assurance that faith brings, having our hearts sprinkled to cleanse us from a guilty conscience and having our bodies washed with pure water."

I was, after intense soul searching, *deep healing through God's scriptures*, and the abounding FAITHFULNESS of Jesus' presence in my Spirit entering into this MOST HOLY PLACE. Knowing to the core of my being…this cleansing and being 'WASHED WITH PURE WATER'; TRULY BEING BORN AGAIN.

CHRIST AWARENESS

Let your light shine!

CHRIST AWARENESS: THERE IS A NEWNESS TO ONE'S LIFE WHEN WE REALIZE WE ARE TO live our lives out of this humility as opposed to self-awareness. I was suddenly seeing my life as one to be lived in Christ's shadow, Him being the light that is a beacon that all around me are drawn to.

Matthew 5:16 (ESV) In the same way, let your light shine before others, so that they may see your good works and give glory to your Father who is in heaven.

For me, during my healing process, being in a place of DARKNESS was commonplace... even while being in a well-lit room. As I processed much evil of my past, at the hands of others, the fear of darkness was almost insurmountable. To me, DARK AND LIGHT could NOT coexist. The light was good, the darkness was bad...even knowing GOD was the creator of all and DID INDEED call it good upon completion. *It wasn't until my expulsion of my turbulent, trauma-filled past was laid to rest that I could escape that DARKNESS INSIDE of me.* Here is where I believe MY LIGHT was never meant to be hidden, *yet much hard work was needed to ALLOW MY LIGHT TO SHINE!*

Matthew 5:14,15 (ESV) "You are the light of the world. A city set on a hill cannot be hidden. Nor do people light a lamp and put it under a basket, but on a stand, and it gives light to all in the house.

John 8:12 (ESV) Again Jesus spoke to them, saying, "I am the light of the world. Whoever follows me will not walk in darkness but will have the light of life." There is no greater feeling than deliverance from the darkness that has been carried, resituated, shifted; yet never released. Once felt, we are NEVER the same. Thank you, God, for allowing me to shine before others, ALL GLORY TO YOU, FATHER.

PRAY ALWAYS

Count your Blessings!

"Rejoice in hope, be patient in tribulation, be constant in prayer." Romans 12:12 (ESV) "Continue steadfastly in prayer, being watchful in it with thanksgiving." Colossians 4:2 (ESV)

I HAVE FOUND MYSELF, NOW, FORWARDING EVEN MY SMALLEST CONCERNS, AND ESPECIALLY deep hurts heavenward. I was always one to try and *'HANDLE'* what life threw at me, I was usually quite adept, and with adequate results. But when it came to the deep wounds, the crushing hurts that lingered in my life, *my efforts seemed futile.*

But with one glance at ALL that God has led me through, all the promises fulfilled, the dark corners of my mind filled with His glorious light; why would I NOT TRUST HIM WITH EVERYTHING? And THAT was the bigger question! ("When my life was fainting away, I remembered the Lord, and my prayer came to you, in your holy temple." Jonah 2:7 ESV) God truly is the ONLY ONE who can set things straight in this upside-down world. Suddenly, every time I felt the flicker of sadness, the sting of an unkind word remembered, the intense pain of an old rejection, or guilt of past confessed sin; my prayers were sent to God's Throneroom. Who better? Sent to the lover of my soul, the One who knows my heart BEST. I was truly feeling, not only softening in my spirit but more forgiveness and *release from the hurt and pain,* which freed up even more space in my body FOR GOD'S GLORIOUS LIGHT!

"Therefore, I tell you, whatever you ask in prayer, believe that you have received it, and it will be yours." Mark 11:24 (ESV) But…what about those times we feel like our prayers are falling on deaf ears? Do we wonder if we are doing it WRONG? Is God NOT LISTENING to us? Many times, I wondered, am I to continue waiting on the LORD? Are my prayers insufficient?

Oswald Chambers might have preached this over 100 years ago, yet it is still true today, "Prayer changes ME and then I change things. God has established things so that prayer, based on redemption, changes the way a person looks at things. Prayer is not a matter of changing things externally, but one of working miracles in a person's inner nature."

We are not to come to Jesus half-heartedly. He did NOT die on that cross for us to half-heartedly follow Him! "We know that for those who love God, all things work together for good for those who are called according to HIS PURPOSE. For those whom He foreknew, He also predestined to be conformed to the image of His Son in order that he might be the firstborn among many brothers. And those whom He predestined He also called, and those whom He called He also justified, and those whom he justified He also glorified." Romans 8:28-30 (ESV)

As I continued to HEAL, THUS CONTINUED TO GROW, I realized my prayers were answered in God's way, certainly not the way I had assumed they SHOULD BE ANSWERED! My way was to skip the HARD parts, all the growth parts. As I read back over Paul's advice, "Rejoicing in HOPE, Being PATIENT in tribulation, as well CONSTANT IN PRAYER… ALL the while STEADFASTLY being WATCHFUL WITH THANKSGIVING. I recount the ways this consistency in prayer, by patience and steadfastness, has given me MUCH TO BE THANKFUL FOR! My faith has grown through the GRACE I was GRANTED through the long-suffering. This led to more time spent in GOD'S HOLY WORD. Blessings abound among those he glorifies. I thank you, FATHER, for shaping me and conforming me more closely to Your Son's image.

COUNT YOUR BLESSINGS

CONSTANT IN PRAYER

As I heal, grow, and watch my prayers being answered, I thank You Lord, for Graces granted.

No. 1

Grace Abounds

REJOICE ALWAYS

Pray Always

What are some of the powerful prayers that I am seeing answered...

& Graces given!

How has this changed me internally?

"Prayer changes ME and then I change things. God has established things so that prayer, on the basis of redemption, changes the way a person looks at things. Prayer is not a matter of changing things externally, but one of working miracles in a person's inner nature."

Oswald Chambers

HUMILITY: THE BEST POSTURE

Grace: holy eyesight

As my body began *filling with this light* and, dare I say, freedom from the demons that have chased me for years, life seemed to take on a new dimension. The absolute and TRUE realization of the GRACE AND MERCY that we receive continually from OUR GLORIOUS GOD seeps in and consumes us. Suddenly, we begin to see the barb sent our way that was meant to strike or disarm us through new eyes: the eyes of GRACE. We don't see the anger or the enemy, we see the SUFFERING or wound of a person. We can now begin to be curious and possibly question perception and miscommunication, theirs and *ours*: Experiencing breakthroughs and solutions instead of broken hearts and broken relationships through grace and mercy.

Ephesians 4:32 (ESV) Be kind to one another, tenderhearted, forgiving one another, as God in Christ forgave you.

Ephesians 5:1,2 (ESV) Therefore, be imitators of God, as beloved children. And walk in love, as Christ loved us and gave himself for us, a fragrant offering and sacrifice to God.

Thank you, God, for this newfound holy grace-filled eyesight and blessings freely given.

STRENGTH FOR TODAY

Start each day new.

For nothing will be impossible with God. Luke 1:37 (ESV)

FOR THOSE OF US WHO HAVE HUSTLED OURSELVES TO EXHAUSTION, 'WAITING ON THE LORD' can be our 'new mantra' to live by. I hear this Exodus verse ringing in my ears, "The LORD will fight for you; you need only to be still." (Exodus 14:14 NIV) Knowing, just as Moses trusted the LORD as he led the Israelites out of Egypt and through the Red Sea, brought water out of rock and 'manna' daily from heaven to feed them: Basically, doing what seemed IMPOSSIBLE! This IS the SAME GOD we worship today. He is just as powerful, pushing us through the impossible: God is our Source and our supply daily. His Presence is our protection. Believing that we, in OUR power, if we just work harder, can fight the tough battles that this fallen world tends to layer on us is unnecessary when we have a God of the impossible. Now to Him who is able to do far more abundantly than all that we ask or think, according to the POWER AT WORK WITHIN US, to Him be glory in the church and in Christ Jesus throughout all generations, forever and ever. Ephesians 3:20-21 (ESV)

Such is the confidence that we have through Christ toward God. Not that we are sufficient in ourselves to claim anything as coming from us, but our sufficiency is from God. (2 Corinthians 3:4,5 ESV)

Learning that ALL that we have comes from and through God frees us tremendously. Living in freedom, being who God created us to be, authentically ourselves, shatters the pretense we previously lived in. Now we can fly above the plastic world of make-believe and attend to matters of the heart: GOD'S HEART. For most, I believe, God's heart leads us to a weightier calling. As much insight is gleaned from our healing, we have gained a new understanding; a discerning Spirit of sorts, and a keen perception to assess the needs of others. This sacrificial recognition and perception, I believe, comes from the Holy Spirit which is shining brightly in us now that we are filled through and through!

"If you desire to make a difference in the world, you must be different from the world." Elaine S. Dalton YES! We must be the 'different' in this world if we are to free others to be their *authentic FREE SELVES.*

Help me, Jesus, *to be the DIFFERENCE.*

Now to Him who is able to do far more abundantly than all that we ask or think, according to the power at work within us, to Him be glory in the church and in Christ Jesus throughout all generations, forever and ever.
Ephesians 3:20-21

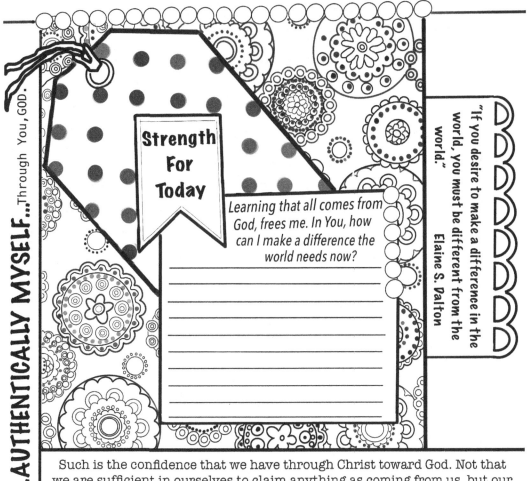

...AUTHENTICALLY MYSELF...Through You, GOD.

Strength For Today

Learning that all comes from God, frees me. In You, how can I make a difference the world needs now?

"If you desire to make a difference in the world, you must be different from the world."
Elaine S. Dalton

Such is the confidence that we have through Christ toward God. Not that we are sufficient in ourselves to claim anything as coming from us, but our sufficiency is from God.
2 Corinthians 3:4-5

As much insight is gleaned from our healing, we have gained a new understanding; a discerning Spirit of sorts, and a keen perception to assess the needs of others. This sacrificial recognition and perception, I believe, comes from the Holy Spirit which is shining brightly in us now that we are filled through and through!   Julie

SPEAK ENCOURAGEMENT

Beautiful minds inspire others.

To be that difference in the world, for me, meant sharing all the JOY and FREEDOM that I had access to once I released all the layers of trauma. The encouragement that I received was instrumental in my journey to healing. I knew this was CRUCIAL: to be supported through the pain and encouraged during the tough times. Many times, when isolation seems our most obvious choice; this is when the reassurance of a friend saves us. TO BE HEARD in our pain and struggle not only holds us buoyant but has a way of fortifying us as well. We feel supported by our champions who hold us when we are too weak to steady ourselves. This is what God calls us to do daily--building *each other up and* bolstering each other in this life of many difficulties.

May the God who gives endurance and encouragement give you the same attitude of mind toward each other that Christ Jesus had. Romans 15:5 (ESV)

I long to see you so that I may impart to you some spiritual gift to make you strong—that is, that you may be mutually encouraged by each other's faith. Romans 1:11-12 (ESV)

Blessed be the God and Father of our Lord Jesus Christ, the Father of mercies and God of ALL COMFORT, who comforts us in all our affliction, so that we may be able to comfort those who are in any affliction, with the comfort with which we ourselves are comforted by God. For as we share abundantly in Christ's suffering, so through Christ, we share abundantly in comfort too. 2 Corinthians 1:3-5 (ESV)

Greater love has no one than this, that someone lay down his life for his friends. John 15:13 (ESV)

Bear one another's burdens, and so fulfill the law of Christ. Galatians 6:2 (ESV)

As I find so much comfort in the words of sacred scripture, this same scripture leads me to a call to action on the part of others. Once again, the SACRIFICIAL LOVE OF CHRIST. Giving of ourselves to bless others which in turn fills us with abounding BLESSINGS. Thank you, God, for the SPIRITUAL GIFT of Your *strength in my weakness*, to encourage others in their walk to freedom from their suffering. Amen.

Beautiful Minds Inspire Others

May the God who gives endurance and encouragement give you the same attitude of mind toward each other that Christ Jesus had.
Romans 15:5

I long to see you so that I may impart to you some spiritual gift to make you strong-that is, that you may be mutually encouraged by each other's faith.
Romans 1:11,12

Write a short 'Prayer of Thanksgiving' for those who have been your Supporting Champions throughout your healing. Who can I 'cheer' for now?

Bear one another's burdens, and so fulfill the law of Christ.
Galatians 6:2

_____
_____
_____
_____
_____
_____
_____
_____
_____
_____
_____
_____
_____

DELIGHT IS A DECISION

The desires of our heart are the gift.

THE LORD YOUR GOD IS WITH YOU, THE MIGHTY WARRIOR WHO SAVES. HE WILL TAKE great delight in you; in His love, He will no longer rebuke you, but He will rejoice over you with singing. (Zephaniah 3:17 ESV) Awesome, He will DELIGHT AND SING *over ME*.

Delight yourself in the Lord and He will give you the desires of your heart. (Psalm 37:4 ESV) Sounds easy enough, right?

To DELIGHT is to gain great pleasure, satisfaction, and happiness; the Hebrew translation; is to be soft or tender. Delighting in this relationship with God, for me, has certainly been a labor of love, but as I had seen, He had truly done most of the heavy lifting. Things were changing though!

As I took a long hard look at my life, I made a conscious decision to DELIGHT in the LORD. I felt led by God to make this life-altering choice. I would delight in His word more deeply. I would trust in His plans for my life more fervently, *regardless of outcomes*. I chose to DELIGHT IN THE EVERYDAY MOMENTS God brought my way. What a beautiful *freedom* for us as we grow in our worship and *delight in His Glorious Nature*, delighting in the pleasure of every moment; a grandchild's eyes as precious time is shared or the cool breeze on a warm summer evening. Being ALL-IN; *DELIGHTING in every good and perfect gift* that He shares with me every moment of my life.

But most importantly, as I'd *GROWN THROUGH* my 'trauma', my mindset seemed to have matured as well. I would meditate on scriptures focusing on *God's DELIGHT IN ME*, as His beloved daughter. I would continue to delight in my Heavenly Father even when I FELT my desires weren't being met or when I FELT as if I'd let Him down in one way or another. *The TRUTH was and is, GOD CONTINUES TO DELIGHT IN ME.*

And…it seemed in all my delighting in THIS GLORIOUS FATHER, God was showing me the desires that I had felt had always lacked in my relationship with my LORD…TO BE TRULY KNOWN, LOVED, AND DESIRED BY GOD. I suddenly realized; I was My Father's HEART'S DESIRE. Blessings ALWAYS abound with GOD!

DELIGHT

♥ LOVED ♥

DELIGHT YOURSELF IN THE LORD, AND HE WILL GIVE YOU THE DESIRES OF YOUR HEART.

PSALM 37:4

THE LORD YOUR GOD IS IN YOUR MIDST, A MIGHTY ONE WHO WILL SAVE; HE WILL REJOICE OVER YOU WITH GLADNESS; HE WILL QUIET YOU BY HIS LOVE; HE WILL EXULT OVER YOU WITH LOUD SINGING.

ZEPHANIAH 3:17

God DELIGHTS in ME!

I AM KNOWN.

Have I focused quiet time delighting in the Lord? Time in His presence is life altering. Do I feel Him delighting in me? He certainly does! _____

_____

_____

_____

_____

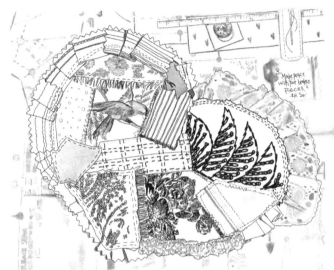

As I find peace and comfort in the words of Sacred Scripture, does my heart feel this 'piecing back together'? Am I delighting in my relationship with My Father? Am I reminding myself often of just how much My Holy Father delights in Me?

_____

_____

_____

_____

_____

_____

_____

The LORD Your God is in your midst, a mighty one who will save; He will rejoice over you with gladness; He will quiet you by His love; He will exult over you with loud singing.

Zephaniah 3:17

GOD IS STILL WRITING MY STORY

And Heaven has a plan.

As GOD CONTINUES TO WRITE THIS NOVEL, THAT IS MY LIFE, I PRAY THAT I CAN HAVE eyes to continually see what the LORD is doing in my life as well as all around me. I remain stubborn in my belief that there is good in this world. I am hopeful that we are all working toward a common goal; GRACE-FILLED LIVES! Lives that lead into the heart of Jesus, being the GOOD, being the JUSTICE, being the KINDNESS that our great IMAGE BEARER, JESUS demonstrated. He exemplified this in a way we can hope to mirror, and WE ARE called to be His representatives, not just admirers.

Knowing that I am ENOUGH; that my OBEDIENCE is all that God asks of me, and with HIS GRACE received, this ask is freely given. God's deep healing, after such soul-wrenching hurt, has certainly strengthened my spirit as well as softened my heart. I now understand this ETERNAL CONNECTION that my heart has with My LORD. The connection is much more than being 'moved' or 'inspired' by my Heavenly Father. It is about coming to Him daily with a repentant heart, eager to accomplish HIS WILL, in HIS STRENGTH, WORKING THROUGH ME. (Search me, O God, and know my heart! Try me and know my thoughts! And see if there be any grievous way in me and lead me in the way everlasting! Psalm 139:23-24 ESV) Once connected to God's heart, the TRUTH of His ways comes into focus. I believe *I will NEVER be the same;* well, I can only hope!

I find myself living life passionately for Christ, now that I know God has given me all the "STRENGTH THAT I NEED FOR ALL MY TOMORROWS!" Now I can build my life on ALL THAT IS 'NEW'; exchanging my heavy yoke of secrecy and oppression for this new yoke which is easy and light. ("Come to me, all who *labor and are heavy laden, and I will give you rest.* Take my yoke upon you, and learn from me, for I am gentle and lowly in heart, and you will find rest for your souls. For my yoke is easy, and my burden is light." Matthew 11:28-30 ESV)

I was blessed to receive much, as my grisly STORM HAD *A PURPOSE*. I see now, how God uses our external circumstances to bring about internal purification. God redeems those storms we go through. We have to leave behind what we know to step into the new. For me, that meant abdicating the demand for justice that would not come, unlocking God's glorious GRACE that led me to the throne. His throne; which judges all, forgives all, and *gives life to all who come to Him.*

I have seen that we must stand with our hands and hearts open, ready to receive all that the Lord wants to impart to us. Even when the 'GIFT' seems painful or unwanted, we must know God is for us ALWAYS. He, like any good parent desires our growth. I have learned through experience, quite possibly the hard way, that *remaining 'curious' and open to growth is scary but a necessity in life if we are to become all that God intends for us.* We are always evolving. Be ready to grow. Be excited. Life is for giving once those gifts are given to us. We are to hold everything loosely in this world…it is not ours, as we are just passing through.

I PRAISE YOU, LORD, FOR HEALING, FREEDOM, AND YOUR GRACE FREELY GIVEN. AMEN.

As she moves further into her healing process grounded firmly in Jesus; this second book reflects her growth. With thanksgiving and praise given to the Holy Sprit working through her process, a newfound freedom brings authenticity and ultimately the peace she has always longed for.

Printed in the United States
by Baker & Taylor Publisher Services